Pigs' Feet, White Socks & Hoovers

Ten Years of Sean O'Faoláin Prize-winning Stories

Southword*editions*

First Published in 2013
by
Southword Editions,
Munster Literature Centre
Frank O'Connor House
84 Douglas Street,
Cork,
Ireland.

www.munsterlit.ie

ISBN 978-1-905002-38-2

Grant Aided by
Cork City Council

Contents

What Slim Boy, O Pyrrha
William Wall

I give you the image of a man running naked into the battle. Not quite naked, because he wears his helmet. Why do we feel he is peculiarly vulnerable? As if his uniform of coarse cloth could protect him against a high velocity rifle-round or a stream of bullets from a Maxim gun. The period, of course, is 1914–1918 – the Maxim gun is the key. Is he an officer or a private soldier? And why is he naked?

Say, his trench has been surprised during the night and now that the initial raid has been repulsed he leads his men in a counter-attack. *Carpe diem!* He shouts to them, although they do not understand the language. *Carpe diem!* He has a battered copy of Horace's *Odes* (Everyman Library Edition) in his kit. He waves his revolver above his head and they grin and say the old man has finally gone bats.

The image has certain engaging qualities: a naked man (under the mushroom-cap of his helmet) stands on the lip of a trench and urges his men to attack in Latin. But they follow him because he is the old man, because he talks to them in some foreign lingo, because he's starkers and he doesn't give a tuppenny damn. They pour over the trench, chuckling affectionately, into the brilliant artificial day of no-man's land and the bullets fly and the star-shells pop and hiss. The men hear the bullets that do not have their names on them whispering suddenly in the air, but nobody hears the bullet that has his name. It nips the jugular, holes the aorta, or slips in above the ear and exits into the helmet set at a jaunty angle filling it with brain.

At some time in the half-hour of this particular battle the naked officer stands above the corpse of a German soldier who has been shot through the eye. Another distressing image. A bullet in the eye is a barbarous wound. The naked man looks down at the one-eyed un-seer.

Now that his sexual organs have come into our field of view, the issue of his sleeping naked arises. It is well-known that officers in the front-line trenches slept in their uniforms. We are familiar with descriptions of the damp dugouts, lit by a single candle, full of the thunder of the cannonade, in which sensitive and insensitive men of various ages sit about and doze, in uniforms of various ranks, the highest usually being a major. The officer who packs Horace's *Odes* before leaving Blighty is also a familiar figure. He may well have started the war with *Odi profanum vulgus,* but will end it, if he survives, with *occidit occidit spes omnis*. The *vulgus* will become closer to him than the people of his own class and he will emerge into civvy-street a hopeless misfit or a revolutionary. He inspires fierce loyalty among his men who refer to him by various insulting names which are, in fact, terms of endearment, such as "The Old Man" or "Mad Harry".

But this beats all. Even his batman is shocked by his appearance on the lips of the trench. They are all looking up at him and from that angle he is an impressive figure, almost sculpted in the heroic mode. He might have graced a pedestal in Rome or Athens. Various comments about his genitalia (are they large or small? Something to come back to later if we have time) that pass along the sap in the few moments before they realise the mad bugger wants them to counter-attack, are silenced by the non-commissioned officers.

But now to explain his nakedness necessitates a deliberate switch in time. We consider the possibility of a nostalgic passage encapsulating the memory of an incident which led him into this aberration and realise immediately (or after a few hundred words) that the effect will be to slow the narrative without adding in any way to the suspense. Nor can he reasonably be expected to begin telling someone a sub-narrative at the height of an attack. This is a story and devices available to novelists – interleaving chapters in a complex time-frame, for example – are not appropriate here. In the end, because I want to get on with it, I type three asterisks and go straight into his memory of the day he said goodbye to a certain woman in Beaulieu (it is pronounced 'Bewley', and, surprisingly, is in the south of England, not France) on a languid summer afternoon in 1914.

* * *

The sun is low on the evening of a perfect day. The cypress trees cast long irregular shadows on the manicured lawn. In the distance the pock of mallet and ball can be heard. (Or perhaps the pock of bat and ball? The villagers have come to the house of the rich man – the lord? – for their annual cricket match against the tenants. They linger in the edge of memory, in white, doing very little for long periods and then rushing about in inexplicable patterns. The whirling arm, the swing of the bat – pock.) Down the cypress walk you go, from shadow to shadow, following the woman and the man. You hear their tender conversation. He wears the uniform of the Hampshire Regiment, and with a gasp you realise that this is the first time in the story that you have seen him with his clothes on. It creates a peculiar kind of intimacy which you find contradictory. At first you see them at a distance, moving elegantly among the trees. Then you approach more closely, and finally you are a secret third party to their conversation, the ghost of the future standing with them, shoulder to shoulder.

It comes as a shock to discover that their conversation is salty and sexual. They are reliving an actual sexual encounter in detail. The language they use is pure D.H. Lawrence. Because you are a ghost you are privy also to the man's actual thoughts and I have given him certain phrases from Catullus and Ovid (we have already established that he is a classicist) which confirm the universality of the terms. But her thoughts are out of bounds because it suits the direction of the narrative to have an inscrutable heroine. She is always other in the story, an object of his thoughts, his memories, his fantasies. And yours. After a time the subtle interplay of the still, warm evening, the gentle sound of the cricket game, the sex and the Latin, create an extraordinary, sensuality, a Mediterranean languor set against the battlefield images with which the story opened. Now the felicity of that switch (indicated merely by the three asterisks) becomes clear. And because we have really moved in time – rather than merely moving into memory –

the detail can be piled up to add to the overall effect. What do they look like? She is tall and slim and moves with a fluid grace. He is taller, thin because he is a scholar, with the stiff back of the stoic (or the officer). He thinks poetically, seamlessly, in several languages, but he speaks haltingly. His words are clipped, uncertain, hesitant. His accent is Anglo-Irish; hers is Swiss finishing school via Cheltenham Ladies' College. When he is required to utter complete sentences he stutters as though he is aware that he is a foreigner in several tongues. He loves her madly, of course. At least this is the way he thinks of it, the precise phrase in fact. When he is away from her he dreams constantly of her body and certain parts of it in particular. Now, as he walks he moves his hand to his face and smells her on it and she laughs because this is a shared joke. She knows where his hand has been. Even at dinner table, or at stilted gatherings in her father's drawing-room, or in a railway carriage, he only has to make the shadow of the same gesture and she smiles. We know she likes to use the most vulgar terms for parts of his body and hers, the coarseness itself exciting her – her face is a little flushed now – and all of this is somehow related, in an extraordinary way, to her elegance and refinement.

They walk side by side but not arm in arm because there is something that prevents them being seen as a couple. In fact, there are two things. Firstly, of course, she is the daughter of a lord, a millionaire who has made his money in the shipping business and now sails a yacht in the same races as King George and the Kaiser. On the other hand he comes from a middle-class family of university teachers, clergymen and scholars. His family may construct the way England thinks (a hundred years before, Ireland too), but England, or at least its rich, use the construction to ignore or despise anybody who thinks at all. Her father has envisioned a marriage of alliance for her, with the son of a man who owns, among other things, a commercial insurance company.

The second impediment is a more subtle one: they are cousins. The term 'scion' is appropriate but vastly over-used in relation to the English nobility, a metaphor drawn from the practice of grafting plants and redolent of a certain vegetable quality in that class. Equally, the term 'distaff side', a metaphor drawn from the manufacture of clothing at cottage industry level, is not entirely appropriate. I leave the construction of the relationship for the re-write. Suffice it to say that he is from the Irish branch of the family which labours under some disgrace incurred during the eighteenth century and which the stern and dour behaviour of six or seven generations has not been sufficient to erase.

They are cousins and therefore the odour of incest permeates their bed. This is an inappropriate and an illegitimate relationship and is therefore doomed.

At this point you realise that the young man will die.

He can never return to find his lover married to a boring fart who drives a Bugatti or a private aeroplane. She would be miserable and he would feel futile. A tragic as opposed to a depressing ending has become a necessity. When we last saw him in the battlefield he was standing (naked still) with his revolver by his side, looking down on a German soldier who had been shot through the eye. We return now. No asterisks are necessary. Perhaps they were not necessary in the first place.

A momentary silence has fallen over the battle-field. His men have seized the enemy trench and so, as usual, the silence indicates that the enemy is re-grouping. In a few moments they will return. In this silence he gazes down at the dead man and various allusions are placed in his mind. He thinks, in fact, about one-eyed monsters and the ill-omens that attend them. He shivers and is suddenly acutely aware that he has no clothes. He looks down at his genitals and wonders did he lose his trousers in the course of the fighting. He has seen a man, stripped bare by the force of an explosion, walk away from a near direct hit by a trench mortar. Then he notices that the physical activity of killing has caused a tumescence, not quite a full erection, but a happy state of engorgement such as exists immediately after coitus. He thinks of the woman he has left behind in Beaulieu and laughs softly.

The counter-attack must be now or never. The very first round fired will strike him in the chest, just slightly to the left of the heart but close enough for the bone splinters to rip it open. He spins and falls. The very simplicity of his nakedness, the apparent savagery of it, the barbarian disregard for the niceties of twentieth century warfare, made him the number one target for German sharpshooters. There is irony in the iron inevitability of it. His revolver and his disregard for his own safety marked him out as an officer. Later he would get a posthumous award for leading the charge and survivors would chuckle over their pints in 1925 and say, If the brass only knew, or, They wouldn't have known where to hang it.

Where to next?

A brother officer, a scholar of the same college at Oxford arrives to gather his effects. The chaps in the dugout (a major is the highest ranking officer) point them out. He was mad they say. He always slept naked. Of course, the CO never mentioned it when he wrote to break the bad news. The major says that he hardly thinks it necessary to bother the poor family with the fact that he was bollocks naked when the Hun got him. Nobody laughs. They all loved him.

In a small notebook, in a pocket of the tunic he never put on, the brother officer finds the following words from Horace's fifth ode of the first book: *quis multa gracilis te puer in rosa/ perfusus liquidis urget odoribus/ gratto pyrrha sub antro.* And in an often-worked translation underneath: What slim boy, O Pyrrha, perfumed and drenched in rose-water, have you pressed into service in your privacy now? From the crossings-out it is clear that he has already translated and rejected certain words in certain ways: 'smells' for odoribus, for example. *Urget* was rendered as 'forcing' at one point and 'ravishing' at another. In particular perfusus liquidis was given, in one version, as 'drenched by your juice'. The brother-officer understands nothing of the background that we have given his friend, but he understands the pain well-enough. And when he finds her letter his understanding is complete. It is, of course, both unnecessary and unworkmanlike to reproduce the contents of the letter in our story, but we can be certain that they would explain why the officer slept naked, went into the battlefield naked and died naked. And so we return to that initial image.

Why is it that the idea of a man going into battle without underwear or a serge jacket seems so abhorrent?

Pilgrims of the Night
Mary Leland

Every community has its secrets, just as it has its river, its wood, its church, its school. In this valley I am one of the secrets, hidden like a stone in an overgrown churchyard. Trees cloak and cloud the hills, and the river cuts through them in a broad swathe. It is a tidal river, and for centuries it was navigable. It brought the monks from Lismore. It brought the Knights from Hospital in Limerick, ending here a journey begun in Jerusalem. Their tower crowns their hill, once a place of pilgrimage.

The monks too left their evidence: the abbey is crumbling back in the rock on the island and in summer the trees conceal it. Yet it is there even though the island is an island no more and reeds and sedges choke the lagoon. Invisibility is not absence. Ghosts grown from things unseen but present. Legends swell from spores of half-forgotten fact, from imagined detail, from secrets spoken in furtive asides, in leers, in knowing, acceptant shrugs, in overheard whispers building to the community of evidence creating an event from a suspicion. Standing above this river now I think of how the Normans perused the Old Irish from Waterford back to Cappoquin. Watching again the sweep with which it folds itself back into the mountains I remember that Strongbow defeated Gilbert son of Turgerius where the river meets the sea at Youghal; escaping Irish boats floundered and were held fast in the mud as the tide sank. On the abbey island a Norman is buried, Raymond le Gros, the great: a friend to Strongbow, an alien who surged up this river a thousand years ago and has never left it.

These were the ghosts of my childhood. I thought like them I would never leave. There are places in the hills on either side from which the captive river can be seen in its glossy curves. The house into which I was born was set—its skeleton still visible beneath its thatch of woodbine and briar—on a terrace cut from the cliff by the river's early glacial course. That house gave our family, gave me, a sense of physical immunity because we were set on an incline, a height above the level of the village just as the village is above the level of the river.

It was not a true distance; how could it be, measured with the eyes of childhood, and of memory? Yet it seemed to me then that this river was a street. We crossed it with oars. We fished it, we swam it , we followed its swathes both to the town and to the sea: to the castled banks of its descent from the western mountains, to the reeded shores where it swelled and strengthened and flooded before it vanished forever beyond the lighthouse. Men went up this river with animals and goods and came home talking of Fermoy and Mallow and Kanturk. Men went down this river with nets, and disappeared.

So did I. Disappearance helps a secret to solidify. Absence is useful. My absence began not at the river quay but in the jolting trap sent to take me with my mother into the town on and the journey to our lives thereafter. Any journey even in a rattling farm cart was momentous; this thrill was two-fold because it was shared with my mother who was never demonstrative, or at least not to me or my brother. I was distinguished, I felt. I had no premonition. Loss would become a new emotion to be learned at my mother's knee but as we swayed into the boreen only the flag of the collie's tail tugged my consciousness into a sense that something else was happening. When the dog fell off at last from his panting canter beside the wheels and faded back into the hedges I clutched, for a minute, at my mother's soft skirt. Her silk dress, I realised. Unusual. I held on.

Sometimes in these past years I would see ducks or swans flying over the city's towers and steeples, navigating without charts the arching cranes and throbbing limitless wires. Never many birds, two or four or five perhaps, and I would watch their slow swerve of alignment with some park of lake hidden to me. Their bodies seemed weighted, the noise of their wings a heavy ponderous sigh. How vulnerable they looked, the sky cast above, the city vast below. Yet they would descent—I knew this even if it would take place where I could not watch—with fragile precision to their home, settling their wings with satisfied, businesslike clucks and siftings, the stirred water composing itself around their breasts.

Under the wild clematis at the cottage I see that the outhouse lintel is still scratched with the names of our pets: the donkey Tankard, Stripey the cat, Sonny the raven found injured and kept alive and malicious by my brother. The childhood inscriptions do not include Blue, the collie with one blue eye, who died, I suppose, after I departed with my mother. I would not have been told. But something came to an end here, I think as I stand like a shadow in the yard and read the empty spaces on the stone.

Interpreting the incisions, blunted like Ogham but decipherable to a longing eye, I am reminded by these memorials of the tablets to the FitzGearlds, the Villers, the Stuarts and the Beresfords whose names and titles are cut into the walls of Dairinis church. The church is closed. Were I to remain I could worship at Cappoquin on alternate Sundays, or at Lismore, or at Youghal in the summer. The congregation would be small. There would be no-one I remember, although there would be people that remember me.

I was not born to Dairnis; I heard it's anthems from childhood and lodged them like ballast in my heart for the freight of Latin hymns learned at school, and love, too, despite my mother's reminders that they were out of place in her company. I had no discrimination. One tune was as good as another in the songbook of my life. The choices suggested by my mother were puzzling, too much for me to interpret. For if I was not born to Dairinis church, she was not born to the cottage which is now crumbling softly back into its genitive clay. I cannot revisit her early life although I wanted to, tried to, many times. There was a shield – I feel the smell of creosote, hot and tacky, when I think of that barrier, pliant as corrugated iron – there was a shield between the before and the after. When I press it aside I can only find the little history of my self.

I was born to a fisherman's family, a fisherman who harvested from the land as well as the sea and used his acres wisely, who bought a few sheep and sold them and did the same with pigs, who bought a field and sold it, who over-wintered came and grew calves in summertime. A fisherman who never sold his boat and who never left his wife. Who with her brought his two children to mass at Gelndine Church in the valley. For a while. A fisherman who, when his wife said she would go again to work in the city did not protest, not even when she said she would bring one of the children, the girl, me, to live with her there.

I cannot know how she justified that arrangement or why he countenanced it. The stories of their generation explain the animosities of sect which may have sundered them but not the mysterious, unreliable elemental agent which brought them together. If I look back as coldly as I can, back to a stooped man whose hard calloused hands were gentle when they touched me something like an ache is prompted into life in my heart. I see those hands, the dark-haired arms unexpectedly pale as they rotate towards and away from his body for the pull on the oars; I sense the sparkle of an eye, I hear a whistle as the collie makes the homecoming leap over the boundary wall or rushes from the shelter of the hydrangea bushes at the gate.

When I was eight years old my father left my life. We were never more than thirty miles apart yet he vanished. At the time I thought it was we who were leaving, my mother and I in the trap sent over from Youghal. Marriages then did not break up, families were broken only by death. Yet I never spoke to my father again, or saw him from any distance closer than once, from a rock on the river bank as his red-keeled boat surged towards the sea. I watched it pass Tuirin and Dromana and Camphire and the quay at Villerstown. I watched it fade on the filling tide, the strong arms evenly working the oars, the prow cutting smoothly through the flood. Cleaving the water as if with a Norman sword. This was extinction, although I could not know it. I thought – if he had looked backwards, he would have seen me. Surely.

Even in a good marriage, as mine has been, histories have to be learned and re-learned. The happiness I made with my husband depended at first on nothing but what we were to one another, or at least what we seemed, what we thought we were. I have thought of those years as something like a house bought in the youth of our marriage as time scattered its seeds on our lives an annex was needed here, a porch there, another bedroom or a window broken out, a fruit plot reverted to lawn, the lawn to easy-care patio. These are the arrangements we make to accept the alterations of life.

Or sometimes I have thought of our marriage as a ship. One of the long old coasters I saw steaming past the roadside lighthouse at Youghal, that white beacon thrusting like a stalagmite from the rocks which at one side tumble to the strand, at the other solidify in a street, and the light circling, circling its yellow questing beam across the harbour. I saw it from the sea. From my father's boat. I must have seen it many time, but that is what I remember as the first, that late calm winter afternoon when something must have made him row us out too far, perhaps a current in the river drove us out into the roads, too far for the small boat with it's single oarsman although my brother, older than I, could ply the oars too. To get back my father had to strive against the surge of the river, the Blackwater with all its tributaries gather, from the Awbeg to the Finisk, the Funcheon the Bride and the Lickey, united and all entering the ocean here where the little boat bounced on the thick ripples.

Was I afraid? In remember awe. It was my first glimpse of distance, not danger. The town was off to our right as I sat in the stem of the boat, the bailing can in my hand, a light scum of water around my bare feet. The lights on the shore built up in glimmering spires. The turret of the lighthouse stood on the rock, the beam countable in its steady trawl, cutting the dark with its blade of light. Behind the hill of the town the sky glowed with deep winter reds and blues, cold, dense with the water it reflected.

My hands were cold. I remember that. I remember the stoic silence of my father and my brother, the smooth creak of the oars in the rowlocks, the hiss of the water as it lifted under the planks. We were making homeward but the night was falling and I knew because I had heard my father say so that in the dark the river as so steeply shore that only the stars showed the way. Once we left the beam of the lighthouse we must use the stars to guide us. I bailed, my hands rigid on the uneven edge of the can.

This was the time for ghosts. The Knights of God gathered on their hill, the Norman warrior in his stone tomb at Molana. Nameless dead in the dungeon at Strancally. The last drifting lights of the town flashed like steel in the water. A flatfish writhed unexpectedly on the timbers. My heart flared. We entered the river and its wooded dark enveloped us. The sky which had been so coloured over the town, so pale over the sea, was thick now and the stars were hidden. A feeling came over me, I shivered, for there it seemed we were in the thrall of something more immense than the open sea with its light watching for us on the rocks, its town awaiting us.

There were towns where we were going: Cappoquin, Aglish, Villierstown, Clashmore – I could unreel them like a fishing-line. There were towers; Rhincrew, Strancally, Tuirin, Mount Stuart of the Decies. Soon we would name the windows showing their lights through the trees. Yet in this deep-set night the driven boat was flailing against the flood coming down under us. If I licked my lips they were salt. My skin was tight, I felt my eyes had been drawn too wide open. I looked up and up but there were no stars to guide us. They had a life of their own, I thought, they were doing other things.

The river had its own life too. I peered for a landfall as if we were some party of explorers. What had been silence was layered with its own accustomed sounds, a splash not made by the slice of our oars, a bark from a dog-fox, the weighted beat of a heron making for the weir. Looking up I saw the clouds opening and a star, two pink or crimson stars burning on the vacant sky. I heard my father's grunt as the boat pulled out of the channel. My brother stilled his oar and the feathered water pimpled my skin. For a moment there was no movement at all except the river tossing us at will. I heard in my head the words of the hymn: Hark! Hark! The boat was packed with listening. Hark! Here are the pilgrims of the night.

When we moved again we were tilting against the slip at Dairinis. We were home. That was my last journey with my father. When he had tied the boat and my brother had taken up the nets and the catch I tried to walk with them but my feet were numb, my legs nerveless. My father lifted me in his arms and carried me to the house where my mother was waiting to blame him.

Like my parents, my brother is dead now, although he need not be, drowning from his own boat. He died unmarried, reclusive, alone, although he need not have been. We did not communicate even in adulthood, we never caught up with each other. It was as if he had retired from that life of which I had been a part. I had let myself indulge in a supposed affinity, thinking we were both victims of decisions made to separate us from one parent or the other. I had been taken away. He had been left behind. I had hoped once that this conjunction of choices—once I understood them and realised that perhaps they could be called betrayals—might help us find our common ground. Even now, a revenant in the yard where the travellers' joy wreathed around the byre, I thought I might have asked him what had happened to Blue.

But there had been another separation: ethnic and final. In the boat, in the dark, I had heard the words of a Protestant hymn. I would never sing aloud in my brother's hearing. When I sang to my father I sang about the Virgin Mary, about flowers of the fairest. If we were pilgrims we were journeying to different shrines. Now that I have lived it out, now that I have returned to displace my own legend I weigh the afterlife on different scales to all that went before. I have lived through the years in which I sought only excuses, not meaning. I think now that perhaps my brother understood better than I had done how sanctions, like secrets, run underground. There is a current beneath the rock which had carried us too far. We had had no stars to guide us. No lighthouse to warn us to that point where at last the river finds the sea and loses itself forever.

The Good Kind
Jon Boilard

When I got back from Mexico she was pissed. She sat in a cold jail for six days because the drugs were in the house that was in her name. They put our kids in foster care. She got fired from her teaching job. Her old man drove down from San Pablo to bail her out. He called me a fucking pendejo. I stayed with Chapo until things cooled off.

She phoned me on my cell and said she wanted a divorce. And she was taking the kids. Over my dead body, but I didn't say it out loud. She called me a fucking drug dealer. She called me worse things than that. I let her give me an earful because I felt bad.

The truth is I would never let her leave me. Not on those terms.

I told her to sit tight and not make ansy hasty decisions. Chapo let me borrow his Thunderbird and I floored it down 80. The kids were back home and they were excited to see me except for Junior because he was old enough to understand what was going on.

The others hugged my legs and Maria threw a frying pan at me. She'd been making my favorite papooses, and chicken and jaón and cheese spilled all over me along with hot oil. Chapo was always surprised at the shit I let her get away with.

I didn't want to hit her. Then she cleaned up and used the first aid kit where my arm was cooked. Junior got it from the bathroom. He was a studious and obedient boy.

Later I told Junior to watch the niños for a while so I could talk to his mother in private. He smart assed me because he thought he was a little man already. It made me proud of him but I still had to show him that he wasn't quite ready for that yet. Then he cried but it was the good kind of cry that doesn't really come out. And there was fear in his eyes but it was the good kind of fear that every son should feel toward his father.

There was rain on Mission Street. We fogged the windows of the Thunderbird with our words. I parked on Twenty Fourth near the BART station and McDonald's. There was a street musician banging bongo drums and a vendor taking a break from selling coconut paletas. He scowled with fat owl eyes and smoked half a cigarette.

She described how they strip searched her, humiliated her. As she spoke it was clear that they had been able to break her down, to get her to say too much, using the kids as leverage. I needed to know exactly what. Then I explained the consequences. She tapped on my chest with her closed fists until I'd had enough. Enough, I said.

She called me a fucking puto. She said she couldn't live this way anymore. I put my hand over her mouth. Hard at first, to shut her up so I could think, come up with a plan, and then soft and I worked my index finger around her perfect lips and the inside of her cheek that was already moist and warm, ready for me. She bit my thumb in a playful way and then she exhaled and put her wrists behind my neck and pulled me toward her.

Ah yes, I whispered, this is how it will always go.

Then she pushed me away like she was having second thoughts. Then she tugged at the beltline of my jeans and climbed on my lap and stuffed me inside her and we bumped up against each other for a few long minutes. Then her back arched against the steering wheel with the suicide knob. My face was on the flesh of her chest and the small gold cross she always wore. She smelled like the caramelized sugar you drizzle over flan.

Afterward we just sat there sticking to each other and breathing.

She said the worst part was that it was going on her permanent record. And she said that her old man and her tíos and her four brothers wanted to run me out of town but I laughed and told her they didn't have the cojones for it. Not one complete set among them. She shot me a bitter sideways glance. She didn't like to hear it but she knew it was true. There are two kinds of men and I was one and they were the other. I told her she'd better talk some sense into them before they did something crazy and regrettable.

I had to get the car back to Chapo. She stared at the plastic dashboard. There was music. That rancheras shit that Chapo liked. He could be such a fucking wetback sometimes. But when the chips were down he was my carnal. Like for something like this. He'd take care of all the details so I would not get my hands dirty. I stroked her hair and called her my little salvatrucha. She smiled half a smile. I think she knew.

She asked me to come inside and say goodbye to the kids but I wanted to beat the traffic. That's what I told her. There was a moment of silence between us that hung heavy like a dusty old manta. Then she got out and held her jacket over her head and tried to dodge the drops that were falling faster now. Her wet skirt was clinging to her ass and she splashed in a puddle. Now when I close my eyes tight I can remember her just like that.

Aidan Harman
The Serpentine Trap

Henry James laid down his pen, his hand cramped after hours of leisurely paced writing. He listened to the voice in his head, measuring the time it took for the words to float into the sequence that did most justice to the impression he wished to convey. Now the day's work was done and he would spend the evening with Percy Jackson. This delightful scion of minor gentry was an engaging young man in whose company Henry felt more and more at ease. It was not only his class that Henry found attractive though that did play a part. Henry did not think himself a snob, but he did feel at home in the company of those who appreciated the finer things in life, who had been bred to an awareness of duty and were bound by custom, tradition and good manners.

More and more people were abandoning these standards, to Henry's regret, even to his mild horror. Percy's chief appeal for Henry lay in his fine features and exquisite sensibility. Such refinement, such delicacy of taste. The young man, nay the boy, had other, earthier attractions that obtruded themselves from time to time. Henry was stirred by these but did not care to reveal how deeply he was touched, wanted to touch. What would the boy think?

He got up from the desk and stood by the window, looking down on the canal. A gondola went by, the gondolier a fine figure, elegant at his polling, oar upthrust against the dying light. He watched the gondola out of sight then went to the bathroom to refresh himself.

He surveyed himself in the mirror and found what he saw good. A breeze had stirred, lifting the miasma that was all too often a stifling feature of the Venetian evening. He strolled along to keep his appointment with Percy as Caspardi's, a new, much talked of establishment about which he was still unsure. There was something a little too garish about the place. The age was rapidly becoming too bright and too loud. There was too much opulence. Restraint was what Henry valued. Control. Things in their place. He thought of Percy's infectious gaiety, his enthusiasms. It would be a challenge and a delight to exercise some light, playful control over the effervescent boy.

*

The food had been fine. Service too had been perfect. The *maitre d'* knew his work and the waiters, one of whom was really quite, quite delightful to the eye, had been attentive but not effusive. Over coffee and cigarettes he and Percy were talking, not for the first time, about the mystery and meaning of life.

"Well I say this is all there is," Percy asserted.

"It is, to be sure, all we can be certain of," Henry said.

"Which is why we must make the most of it. There are no second chances."

"I'm not sure I agree. We do get an opportunity to start over," Henry said, laying his cigarette down.

"Oh, it's never the same, Henry," Percy said. "You have to seize the moment."

Henry looked slightly alarmed. The idea of violent action like seizure struck him as grotesque. Seizure was not his way at all. Enthusiasm is well enough, but seizure?

"Oh, my dear boy, I simply cannot agree. You cannot make a dash at life as though it were a short and rapid race."

"Sometimes it is," Percy said, "and far more rapid than we realise."

"Oh no. It is a long and measured journey for the most part. You need to pace yourself and ensure that you are not out of breath. It is pitiful to be left gasping in mid course."

"Nonsense," Percy said. "Think back. How many times did you imagine that you had all the time in the world? Then the moment, the person, the opportunity is gone."

"Ah youth. Such impetuosity."

"I don't think you were ever young, Henry." Percy's tone was tender.

"Maybe not," Henry agreed. "I seem to have come to life with a cautious disposition. Mine is perhaps not the best way. But it is the only way I know."

"We can all learn other ways."

"Only if we think them worth learning. For me it is too late."

"It's never too late, Henry. You have only to reach out for life and grasp it."

Grasp! So much energy, so much resolution lay behind the suggestion. Like seizure, it both attracted and frightened Henry. There was too great a degree of decisiveness to make him feel comfortable. Percy was so transformed by the words. He radiated energy. He seemed to be so worthy of being grasped, to invite seizure. If only, Henry thought, but he cut the idea off. Never. The boy would take fright and flight, repelled.

Percy gazed adoringly at Henry, willing him to act, to say or do something, anything to show that he cared. Ought he make some move? Not too subtle, some gesture perhaps, some posture that would make clear just how much he desired Henry and was willing, eager, to oblige him. Should he follow his own advice to Henry? Rush in and risk losing him? That might be better than permanent uncertainty. Percy felt time passing with all the keenness of his twenty five years. Henry seemed to be moving at a different pace, in another world. It was puzzling, frustrating. He must act. He rehearsed an appropriate sentence. *You know how much you mean to me, Henry, how much I value our friendship, our intimacy, our, dare I say it, love.* Yes, that was the way to go.

Mrs Emmeline Travers, a large American lady loomed over them.

"My dear Henry," she brayed, her voice resonant and carrying, her accent unmistakably and unashamedly mid western American.

"Why Emmy!" Henry rose and gave her a courtly bow. Cursing the woman, Percy also rose and waited to be introduced.

With his usual ceremoniousness, Henry did the honours.

"Another young friend, Henry," Mrs Travers boomed. "How devoted you are to the young."

Henry smiled uneasily.

"You must call me, Henry. I'm at the Grand."

"Delighted," Henry said "I'll send a note."

"Oh no ceremony, Henry. Drop in any morning around eleven. We'll have coffee."

And she was gone. So too, Percy reflected with some bitterness, was his moment. The rehearsed sentence would have to wait.

*

Percy Jackson was confiding to his friend Aubrey Mortimer. "He infuriates me. He has to be as mad for it as I am. Think of all that pent up energy. If only he'd come to the point. "

"But he never does," Aubrey said. "That's his hallmark."

"Oh that's just in the writing," Percy said. "Not in real life."

"For Henry writing is the real life. I like his novels but I am not drawn to the courtly old queen, as you are. His trouble is that he is a virgin queen." Aubrey laughed. "You'll have your work cut out for you if you want to penetrate Henry's defences."

Percy knew that Aubrey was right. There was a spinsterish quality to Henry, more marked since he had shaved off his beard. It was a little unsettling.

"Treat Henry as you would your aunts," Aubrey said. "You know how they like to be shocked despite all their protestations of modesty and decorum."

"That might do it," Percy agreed. He looked at Aubrey closely. He really was a sharp fellow, adept at winning and keeping the favours of any number of old gentlemen. Percy would think of Henry was an aunt and see if he might not shock him into action.

*

Henry rifled through the papers on his desk. He was making no progress at all. The story was mired and sinking. Dramatise! was his watchword but he felt lethargic. He was constipated again and the inner sluggishness had taken hold of his mind. He turned to his notebook to sketch out some thoughts on Percy. So ardent, so impetuous, free in his offer of himself, clearly devoted and unquestionably discreet. But Henry hesitated. Hesitation might, he thought, be the motto for his entire life. He was forever drawing back. It was fear of engaging, of committing. He thought of all those looks for all those men down all the years. On his walks through London how often had he seen those looks. The furtive glances from respectable young, and not so young, men. The bolder stares for lower class lads, stares accompanied by a knowing grin. Oh they knew alright. Better than he did himself. But he had held back. The practical aspects of a possible encounter filled him with alarm. It was not that he could not imagine such an encounter. He could imagine it all too well. His imagination forestalled him, filled him with apprehension. The prospect of contact, of intimacy, was too much a thing of his mind and not enough of his emotion. An excess of rationality kept him frozen and indecisive. I have been too long weaving with words, he thought. Life has become a secondary thing for me. Expressing it, encapsulating it, hinting at it, creating it, all these have taken me over. I have failed at living.

On the surface he lived quite well. He dined out, travelled, talked. He was good company. He had a sly wit hidden under layers of subtle expression. Apart from this inner life of the imagination, there was nothing. He was as hollow as the creatures he imagined, women and men who thronged his tales and populated his novels. Like them he was at the mercy of a puppet master. Unlike them, he could not be galvanised into movement. He needed someone to give him the push to get him started.

Hendrik had not managed it. Nor had Morton Fullerton, whose energy, siphoned off by both women and men, seemed prodigious. Perhaps Percy was the one? Could he yield to the boy's manipulation? Put himself into his hands? In his arms?

He stood up and went to the window. No gondola went by to offer momentary distraction. It was time for afternoon tea. Today he would take it alone. He heard far off the doorbell and knew, before he was announced, that Percy had called for tea. Ah well! He went down to greet the attractive young man, who held, it now seemed to him, his fate in his hands.

*

Henry was back at his desk. Nowhere did he feel more at home. Nowhere offered as much comfort, pleasure and reward. He was writing as fast as he could move his pen. The *donneé* had come to him fully formed. All he had to do was give it expression. At moments like this the hand the mere (all too often the sadly inadequate) servant of the mind. Once again he toyed with the idea of dictation. Lets the words flow, as well as they would through his slight speech impediment. He covered page after page, carefully numbered as he went, allowing space for later insertions which he know would inevitably follow. First drafts could only catch the barest outline, but once they were safely written down there was ample opportunity to seek in the crevices of his mind for more detail. For now he had his angle. He had found his way in and today thoughts of Percy or any other young man were far from his mind. Today there would be no going to the window in the hope of the distraction of a gondola. Distraction was the last thing he wanted now. He has left orders with Franco that he is not in to any callers. This would ensure that he would not be disturbed. He could give himself up with total absorption in his work. This was when he felt most fully alive and the mere business of 'life' was not to be allowed to interfere with it in any way.

*

Percy, turned back by a resolute Franco, knew that Henry was in, writing. He knew better to insist or make a scene.

"Tell him I called, Franco."

"Of course, Signor. He will be desolate to have missed you," Franco added with a degree of flourish that underlined the falseness of what he was saying.

Henry was lucky, Percy thought, and realized at once that it had nothing to do with luck. However he might dither in other matters, when it came to his work Henry was resolute, ruthless. It was where he exercised his considerable talent for concentration. And while he was writing the world was kept at bay. The work when completed might be read or not. But while the work was in progress, Henry's life was suspended. The key to Henry's character began to suggest itself to Percy. It was pointless to urge him to relax, to take it say, to 'live'. For Henry writing was living. What had to be done was to persuade Henry that a new emotional experience, of the kind that Percy was offering, would enrich the writing, both broadening and deepening it at the same time. Such an approach required subtlety itself, as did anything that concerned Henry. As he strolled to Florian's to view the waiters, Percy decided that his previous tactics had been wrong in suggesting a break from routine. By the time he reached the café he was in a buoyant mood. He asked for pen and paper and sent a note at once to Henry, proposing dinner in his rooms, that evening. Then he relaxed over his coffee and kept an appreciative eye on the new young waiter, Gianni, who was so wonderfully beautiful that he might have come from the brush of Caravaggio.

*

"My dear boy," Henry said, "you make too much of it."

The meal was over and Franco had withdrawn. Percy sat opposite the writer, wondering how anyone so intelligent, so subtly aware of the motivations of people, could be blind to what lay right before him. It was not unknown, but for a man like Henry James? Short of exposing himself to him, telling him what he wanted them to do together, Percy did not know how to proceed.

A coarser sensibility would have made such an exposure. The likely reaction to it would put an end to the intimacy Percy craved and which, he was convinced, Henry desired. Shock tactics would not work. Henry was armoured in courtesy, so wound about by circuitous and reirculating expression that he resembled a maze, the heart of which was always just out of reach. Maybe shock tactics were the only way after all. No possibility of doubt or misunderstanding. Reveal the matter in, as it were, all its naked force. Percy smiled and Henry raised an eye brow.

"If only you knew what just passed through my mind," Percy said.

"Perhaps I can guess."

"Then try."

"I imagine that you are wondering how long more you can bear to put up with my evasions."

Percy made to speak, but Henry raised his hand, imperious, silencing him.

"I know you think I am playing some elaborate game with you, conducting some bizarre experiment. Such is not the case. I am in the grip of a strange malaise. Like Hamlet, I am given to delay and analysis. It is a temperamental thing. It has always been there and has over the years become more pronounced, so that what was once a useful tool is now an end in itself. I do so enjoy it, you see. My brother, William, insists that I have brought the principle of postponed pleasure to its highest possible manifestation and now worship at it as at an altar. A strange idea from a man with agnostic views. I think however that he may be right about me. It is the delay, the doubt, the postponement that I enjoy. I realize this is not the case with most people. Quite the contrary. So it is that I have lost friends, especially young friends, who, with the impatience and impetuosity of the young, give me up as a bad job. I won't be at all surprised, my dear Percy, to lose you. I will," he said, laying a hand on Percy's knee, "be very, very sorry to do so."

Percy savoured the gentle pressure of the hand, his body stirring ever so slightly, then settling again. It was over, it seemed. This was as clear a no as he was ever likely to get. He stood up.

"At least see what you might have had, Henry," he said, and rapidly unbuttoned his trousers and brought out his barley tumescent member.

"Wonderful," Henry said, gazing at it, making no move other than a slight movement of his buttocks. "Really quite, quite marvellous."

Percy stood exposed for another moment and then, conscious of how foolish he must look, buttoned himself up.

"And now I really must go, Henry," he said.

"Oh must you? You need feel no shame, my boy."

"I don't," Percy said. "I'm afraid all I feel, Henry, is pity."

"Pity?"

"Pity for you. And for me. It might have been so wonderful for us if we could have shared."

"But we have, dear boy. And it has been wonderful. Your generosity just now –"

"That was just a glimpse of what could be."

"And such a glimpse! Such an enthralling sight!"

Percy noticed how excited Henry was becoming. He liked to watch. A voyeur! That as the key to it all. Would he, Percy wondered, like to witness a spectacle? He sat down.

"Perhaps I can stay another while then," he said. It was time to float the idea that Henry might like to spend an evening with himself and his young friend, Aubrey Mortimer.

El Dorado

James Moynihan

On Monday she asked him how he was doing. She thought there was something stuck to his chin. He said, "And do you think I give a rat's ass what you think of my face? I couldn't care less, Ann! Couldn't care less what you think. About anything. I've been coming here for three years now, you pretend not to know me, and that's fine. You've been pretending not to know me since high school, ever since mighty Frank Whiffle cast his stinking eye on you and you walked away. You walked away. So don't give me any of your 'let me wipe that food off your nose' thing now! I don't care what's on my nose. You didn't care if I had a nose for thirty years until this morning! What's your game, Ann? Because I don't care!"

On Tuesday night Ann wondered what got into her. She told herself she didn't do it on purpose. She stared at herself in the mirror and then focused away to the left. Some part of her mind was saying, 'You stupid, you stupid girl!' But she didn't let it speak. She left the bathroom, went to the bedroom, and switched out the light.

She stopped at his table and told him about the divorce on Wednesday. He was quiet. He pushed the coffee cup and saucer away toward the far corner of the table and flicked some crumbs into the palm of his left hand with his small finger. He was thinking, 'Maybe this is what I've been waiting for,' and, 'No, this is none of my business.'

On the third Monday in July, he said, "Maybe you don't need any distractions right now with the thing going on and all but maybe, I thought we could go for a drive or something, take your mind off the lawyers? Out in the country looks pretty good these days. Maybe we could go out the turnpike?"

On Saturday, he drove up Colonial Avenue in his shining dark red 1975 Cadillac El Dorado and parked outside her house. Bright sunshine bounced off the blank wall of the white triple-decker. He liked how she looked as she came down the steps outside the house. She wore a long red dress and carried a small blue cooler.

She put the cooler in the back seat and sat into the passenger side. She did not put on her seat belt. In his head he ran through the little speech he was going to give her about how he used to walk down along Furnace Brook Parkway at night when they were in high school because he found her father's address in the phone book, but he never did call her up because…

He didn't say anything.

And they said nothing up Route 93 and onto the Massachusetts Turnpike. They said nothing all the way through Natick and Framingham, and they said nothing into Worcester, and they said nothing on into western Massachusetts. She thought about saying she liked saying nothing. She didn't say sorry about Marie, or ask him about his kids. She didn't say anything about the weather, even when the sky got cloudy coming into Sturbridge. She knew he had three children and five grandchildren. She had one grown son and a divorce going on.

He slowed down for the exit at the rest area near Sturbridge and said, "We need gas." He pulled in beside the pump and got out.

She said, "I need to powder my nose, honey."

Honey! He remembered her laughing at something he said in French class in 1961. They looked at each other for about two tenths of a second again now. He saw the dry, puffy bags under her eyes, the wrinkles. She saw the gray hair swept back on his head, the double chin. She clambered out of the car and stepped into the service station. He pulled his wallet out of his pocket and looked down at it.

They drove north on the state roads for about another forty minutes before pulling into the parking lot of a restaurant. He held the door open for her and then they waited for a table. They got seated near the window, a waiter handed them the menus and they started to read. They both started to talk at the same moment. She started to say, "When did Marie pass away?"

He started to say, "How is your kid doing?"

Then he said, "You go ahead."

"How long has it been since Marie…"

He looked at his watch and said, "Two years ago in January. So that'd make it, what, ah, twenty nine months?"

He tapped the spine of his menu on the edge of the table. She noticed the size of his hands. They were hard-working man's hands. The fingers were big, heavy and curved. She said, "You were going to ask me something."

He put the menu down and said, "I was just wondering about your kid. You have one, right?"

"Yeah."

"You don't want to talk about your son?"

"No."

"OK then."

She stared down at her menu.

He said, "I don't think it's actually going to rain today. It's hotter than they were saying on TV."

"Good."

He asked, "Do you want to talk about anything?"

Without raising her head she said, "You couldn't spell my name."

He blurted out "What?" along with part of the bread roll he was chewing. "What did you just say?"

"Our names were one line apart on the class roster for French. Do you remember, we had to sign a sheet every day we had French? Our names were printed on the sheet and we had to sign? Your name was Ford, and then there was Paula Fulham, and then there was me; we were separated by one line, and every day I signed one of those sheets I looked at your line to see your signature. It made me feel good. But then, when you were raising money for the Healy Fund, you asked me to spell my name. You hadn't noticed how my name was spelled. And that's why I went to the party at

Klein's with Frank Whiffle."

"Jesus Christ, Ann! That's the craziest thing I ever heard."

He stared at the hair on the top of her lowered head for a minute. Then he shook his head and whispered, "Damn!"

Ann wanted to get all the confession finished as quickly as possible. To the table she said, "There is something wrong with my brain."

He was about to agree, but she continued, "I've had a series of small strokes. Dr. Koronitzer says they will probably keep happening. I can't close my right eye properly any more. It's because of something I was born with. I don't want to be a vegetable. I want to get my divorce. And then I want to commit suicide. I do not want to be a vegetable."

He stared out the window. She eventually raised her head and stared out the window too. If their gazes had been flashlight beams they would've met and crossed paths in the warm air two feet outside the glass.

"Ann, it's not too late, maybe they'll find a cure?"

She didn't answer.

He raised his hand to catch the attention of the waiter.

They drove another few miles and pulled onto a gravel track. At the end there was a space, and a pattern of concrete squares and rectangles lay embedded in the ground.

He told her, "This is my son's – their holiday home."

They walked around the construction site, looked at the view, tried to guess which rooms were going to be what. He looked into a drainpipe.

"They're due to pour concrete here this week, apparently. Isn't it funny? I think this is all sort of futile. My son and his wife, they're good kids, but they think this'll be permanent. They act like they'll be coming up here forever. But when I look at all this work, money and savings they're pouring into it, I just see the day when it all falls apart. This may still be the best thing for them – it's nice around here in the summer and the kids will like it and all that. But some day they're going to find they're restricted in some way, and then maintaining two houses will become too much for them and... I don't know."

She sat back in the car. "Looks like I shouldn't have bothered with my cooler."

"What?"

"I said we forgot to eat the lunch I packed. I clean forgot about it."

As they coasted away down the path, the big old El Dorado creaked, and the wheels crunched the gravel. They left the woods, stopped for traffic at the road, and he asked, "Why do you want to kill yourself, Ann?"

"Because it's over? Because I don't want the last thing I hear in this world to be my son pretending to be heartbroken when everybody's just waiting for me to be gone? Because nobody loves me?"

He started to sing, "Nobody loves me
Everybody hates me
Guess I'll go eat worms
Big fat juicy ones
Little bitty skinny ones
Gosh how they do squirm."

She did not laugh at the song. "I'm serious, I will do it. In my place it actually is a rational decision. I don't want to lie around waiting to die. Look at Hemingway, that's the way to go. I saw my next-door neighbor's aunt dying over the past ten years. She had one big stroke. Then she fell up on the stove and her hands were no good and it was really pathetic. And she was like that for seven years – down at Riverdale Farms. I'm going to send nice letters to everyone I know and then get gone."

He turned onto the ramp for the turnpike. "What if you forget someone?"

"Well, I'll write a general one too. You've all been very good to me. Thanks a bunch, have a nice life. Take it easy!"

"What about Frank?"

"Frank? He'll be happy."

She grabbed Andrew's shoulder. "We've got to go back."

He smiled and glanced at her. "No can do. Stepping back in time, that's a no-no."

"No, we have to go back to the lot, your son's lot – the birds – they're nesting."

"So?"

"I'll show you. Turn around."

They got off at the next exit, which was four miles away, got back on the highway westbound, got back to the gravel path and parked near the construction site.

After about ten minutes waiting, Andrew said, "I don't know Ann, are you sure you're not imagining things?"

She whispered, "Wait."

They listened to the wind high in the trees. And eventually a mourning dove appeared on the edge of a board that was propped against a stack of blocks. It fluttered down behind the stack.

"You see, they're building in there. Their universe will be shattered this week if we don't get them to move on and build somewhere else."

They observed the birds' movements for a few minutes. Then they got out of the car, found the nest behind a plank, and scattered its material – twigs, grass, hair – a few yards away.

Ann spoke to the birds. "I'm sorry we had to do that. It's for your own good. Big bad things will happen here this week. Go and build somewhere else. There's a whole lot of space around here. Move away, live free!"

They drove back to the highway through the sultry afternoon, and as they sped up, Ann said, "My son is getting married."

"OK, is that alright with you?"

"Yeah, it is, Rhonda is nice; she's some sort of a manager at a chemical company or something. But it's a lot of change right now. Frank is moving out, I'm committing suicide, my son's getting married. I'm not sure I can handle it all."

"Yeah, how are you going to attend the funeral? Did you ever think of that? And does the funeral happen before or after the wedding? So many questions, so little time! And red wine, don't forget the red wine. And olive oil."

"You're losing me here, Andrew."

"Marie's uncle was a doctor. He's ninety years old now, and he says that if we all ate no oils but olive oil and we all had a glass of red wine every night, we would none of us ever have a heart attack or a stroke. He says it's just like the engine of a car. If you put grease in there instead of nice clean engine oil, it'll gum up pretty bad. I'd like to show you the inside of the engine in this baby. She's almost thirty years old and clean as a whistle. I change the oil every thousand miles."

The traffic was getting heavy. Ann looked at the other cars. She liked to look at their drivers and then look away before they noticed her stare.

They drove for nearly three hours in silence again until they pulled off the highway in Lexington. They parked in a shopping plaza near some pine trees.

She said, "You must be tired."

"No, I'm OK. It was a nice bunch of quiet passengers. That makes all the difference."

"I wasn't driving at all and I feel exhausted."

Andrew leaned close to her and looked in her eyes. "Ann, I have some bad news for you. You've had a series of small strokes. That might make you tired. Some days. Now, don't you worry, there's things we can do. For example, now, I'm going to get us a boatload of red wine and a fucking truckload of olives – 'be right back after these messages – don't touch that dial!'"

He went into the store.

She looked at the red evening sky. Andrew had left the engine running and the air conditioning on.

Ann put her window down and then reached over to cut the engine. Heat and the rattle of cicadas saturated the air. She thought about her son's wedding, and the noise seemed to get louder. She laid her head back on the edge of the seat, looked up at the darkening sky, and closed her eyes. Drops emerged from the corner of her right eye. They drained down to the hair at her temple and soaked her ear. She was falling into sleep – sleep like a bath of warm oil. She felt herself floating – drifting away – lost in the long wave of insect noise.

Deirdre Jacobson
Gone

"So what happened?" He's stitching up her left hand now – this after he pried it open and tweezed the mirror out. She doesn't answer, feeling her face float, her ears displaced. She's too far down in the well. Besides, the answer belongs to her. Everything's coming in at different angles and depths... The catgut sliding through her hand, the ssntt-ssntt of the scissors, her eye looking back at her from the shard on the tray... This intern doesn't pursue his question, too rapt in his skin tailoring. Good.

She notices that the mirror piece broke roughly into the shape of an arrowhead. Fancy that. She used to collect arrowheads, had brought her favorite with her when she came to New York. On the bus she'd sat by the window, watching the highway unravel: leafless trees repeating themselves; flying crosses on flying churches (of God, of the Nazarene, of the First Baptists, Southern Baptists, Methodists, Pentecostals, on and on forever amen); a polecat carcass; the N&W coal trains; the New River; Herless's filling station; the Kroger's; the Celanese; the tannery; Orange Crush signs nailed to gray barns; the big electric Christmas star up on Ferguson Hill; houses, porches, beagles, trailers, the frost; the fences... and the mountains, stark with winter, sliding by in a great chain of earth bells, holding their tongues as always and taking miles to relent. Her mind had wheeled on while the road kept running away, while everything peeled off and left her naked but for the arrowhead she held awake in her hand…

A touch of breeze blew that morning. The same one, she believed, that had led her to him. Outside the Price Creek town Trailways station she stood next to her suitcase, shifting from one foot to the other to keep from freezing. Although she knew that she'd be able to stand the cold for only a few minutes, she stuck it out, trying to keep from being noticed too much. Already, when she'd come in to buy a ticket, the clerk had asked, "You any kin to Lawson Spangler?" She'd said no, but wasn't sure she'd lied. Now, looking out at the mountains that rose from the railroad tracks on the other side of the New River, she flexed her toes over the money in her left shoe, standing intermittently on three hundred dollars.

The other three hundred lay under her mother's coffee cup on the kitchen table. In front of the cup lay the note she'd written. The latter was useless, she supposed, since she couldn't even explain to herself why she had to run – now, after all that had happened – but she did it anyway, somehow the gesture being more the point.

Except for her leaving with the intention of not coming back, this morning had been the same as any other. The banty crowed before light, as he always did, and then on and on as the dark drained away. And while Paula dressed in her heaviest clothes and quietly packed the old suitcase she'd decided to steal for a while, Ruby never once woke. This was no different either, and Paula was grateful. Hilled up tight under her quilt in winter, as she was now, or sprawled coverless in summer, Ruby could be depended on to sleep deep, her breath taking long strides from her refuge of fathoms. Before Paula left the room, she touched her sister's hair. "Goodbye, Copperhead," she whispered.

Asa was a light sleeper, so when she reached her brothers' door, she touched the wood and thought their names through it: Asa. Clay. She touched her mother's door, too, but there she allowed nothing else, either whispered or silent.

As she was writing in the kitchen, she remembered that he had done the same thing before he left. Her mother had found the note later – after Paula had found him. "Row, don't read it now," Ma McCoy had said. "You got all you can stand." But Roweena, not to be stinted on or denied her grief, was already reaching for the windowsill for it. His wedding band – the only gold he'd ever owned – dropped from the envelope into her palm, as if to remind her of that first promise he'd made when they were young and the future seemed to stretch long and green. Then she pulled out the note and read his second and final promise: "I'm gone," he said.

She'd had a story in case she'd needed one: the truck broke down this morning, and she was heading over to the Ganoes to get a ride with Will. The suitcase, that was empty. A while back, Janie Ganoe had wanted to give Roweena a bunch of Bettina's outgrown clothes for Ruby. There had been too many to put in the paper bags from Kroger's, so she'd just sent them over in the suitcase. Now Roweena was sending it back by Paula. The part about Janie Ganoe was true, but Paula was taking the suitcase. She'd mail Janie money for it when she could, but right then all she'd wanted was to get down the mountain without getting caught.

Punching her boots through snow crust and calluses of ice, she tried not to think much past her next step. But she didn't count on the breeze. At first, she ignored it, even though it cherried her ears and made them sting. Then it tricked her into drawing her eyes toward the hickory behind the barbed-wire fence on her left. From one of the tree's limbs, a branch dangled by a strip a bark and began to sway. Just a little, but it was enough. Enough to pull the hair trigger in her brain and start the creaking in the orchard. Next, the light snow, flakes drifting down like feathers on the small ill wind leading her on. Next, no. Yes, next. Next, the ground clenching her feet, she can't lift them, can't move. Again, the creaking. Can't move. The snow feathers on the small ill wind. Next, no. Yes, next. Next, his feet, Sunday shoeshine, swaying softly, slowly. Next, no. Yes, next. Next his body, wedding-funeral suit, rocking. When the bough breaks. Next –

Down she fell, the road proving to be kind. If it hadn't made her slip, her legs would be walking but she would still be trapped in the orchard inside her head, unable to stop the procession of Next. Nothing seemed to hurt when she got up. There was only a mild ache in her hands, and, after her trembling ebbed, she was able to brush the snow off her clothes and pick up the suitcase. She tried a step. Another. Yes, she could still move.

As she walked, the motion and rhythm calmed her so that she could distil herself to the act of just going, taking respite in the mantra of her feet. She made her way like this for some time, until finally the road began to tilt. With hope and fear climbing inside her chest, she descended warily, and then distraction came again – this time as a relief. This time, the thought came to her that her people must be kin to the road, that she, too, must be related to it, since she was kin to her people. Her people, she thought, tilted just as the road did here, slanting like tipped scales whether they moved up the mountain or down. What, she wondered, would come of her carrying that slant with her to a place of new dimensions?

"You gonna freeze out here, little girl."

The voice's owner offered a stained grin as his lips pulled back and revealed some of the Red Man sitting in his cheek. The bulge of chaw was the only fat thing about him. Life had whittled on and paled him, it seemed; his clothes hung on him like wash draping a dead pine, and the colors of the tobacco pouch that poked up partway from his left coat pocket gave his appearance its only brightness. Where had he come from? Paula hadn't seen him in the station. He was at once a stranger and someone she recognized. He could have been any one of her Spangler uncles or a familiar sent to beckon her back. Either way, when she looked at him she saw two things: he meant kindness, and she would have to be hard against it. Knowing that made her feel lonely as a bone, flesh-cleaned and marrowless. And yet, she did what she had to do. Unsmiling, she told him that she needed some air outside for a while, then looked down quickly at her money shoe, hoping that would be enough.

"Well, it's your frostbite, sister." A little bit of hurt in his tone and a long spit of juice to the ground, but he turned away and went into the station. Now what? How would she avoid him? She'd have to go in, too. Not yet, but soon. She didn't know how much longer she could take the cold. What if he got on the same bus as she did? To ward off the stiffening in her hands, she flexed them in her coat pockets, and, in doing so, her right hand grazed the arrowhead. She held it in her fist, and the edges pressed against her skin.

She was eight when she'd found it pointing out of a furrow in Ma Spangler's field. Most likely Cherokee, he'd said. Probably from a camp here or somewhere nearabouts. Used to hunt and fight in these woods. Lived in Narrowland long before it was Narrowland. She'd taken the arrowhead home, washed it carefully, and put it on the windowsill in her room so that it could dry in the sun. Later, in the evening, she'd put it in the box that her Sunday-school Bible had come in.

That first arrowhead had not begun the romance, however; it had simply vectored it on. Paula had been in love with her idea of Indian people ever since she could remember. And though she had yet to meet or know any of them, like most good romantics, she hadn't let that come between her and how she imagined them to be. She would sit cross-legged on the floor, in front of the small portable TV with its tin-foil-tipped rabbit ears and two snowy channels, and watch the movie Indians meet their fate in black and white. Ready to fight, they would appear on horseback, lining the horizon of a hill with their silhouettes. Then the chief would give a signal with his lance, and the warriors would cascade down as their tremoloed cries shivered up. She'd pretend she was riding with them and always pulled for them to win, regardless of plot, and always she would be disappointed. Often, he watched the movies with her. He, too, would be disappointed when the movie made the warriors lose, despite his knowing better than she what to expect.

Still, the real Indians had won sometimes, and – perhaps to console or warn her, perhaps to do both – he'd told her about one particular victory. At Little Bighorn, he'd said. Sitting Bull, Crazy Horse, and them other fellers – they won the battle but lost the war. She wouldn't understand what he meant till she was older. Had no idea of the carnage involved. After all, reports of real dead soldiers came nightly from the same screen the movie Indians died on. What had mattered to Paula then was that, at least on one day, despite what they had known or guessed about their darkening future, the warriors had fought anyway. They had won, and they were not movie Indians.

Not long after Paula found the first arrowhead, her class had gone to the school library. Usually, she would look for a collection of fairy tales or horror stories, something with plenty of monsters to redeem, outtrick, or outrun. But this time, she'd chosen a book about the Cherokees. It said that they used to live in places from the mountains of Narrowland County, Virginia, all the way down to Alabama. But in the 1838 the president forced most of them to leave what land was still theirs and go to Oklahoma in the middle of winter. They walked a road called the Trail of Tears to get there, and nearly four thousand of them died along the way.

She'd shown him the book, too, and watched him as he read a few pages at the kitchen table, taking long drags off his Viceroy. The tips of his forefinger and thumb were stained a yellowish brown that reminded her of locusts. Andy Jackson. I remember reading in a school book about him. Said he was so tough that people back in them days called him "Old Hickory". Your granddaddy Spangler used to cut switches and sticks off a hickory, called it the "whipping tree." Feller named after something like that must've been meaner than a snake. Blowing smoke out through his nostrils, he'd grinned his best Johnny Cash sneer, then winked at her. Not as mean as me, though, he'd said. Paula had laughed. He could be like that. Once, when he was bantering with Asa, he'd told her brother, Boy, I'm so mean I have to hold a gun on myself to keep from cutting my throat shaving. He liked to play the boogeyman.

In just the past few minutes, the cold had turned glazier, so that any movement of Paula's seemed capable of shattering the air. Finally, she gave in. Picking up her suitcase, she went back inside the station and looked for a place to thaw. With relief, she spotted the Red Man chewer wringing a mop over a bucket. At least he would not be getting on the bus. When he looked up, she noticed his chaw was gone, which afforded him a slight smirk when he saw her.

Moving toward the waiting area on her left, she scanned the rows of benches flanking the central aisle. Long, dark, and pewlike, they underlined in wood how hard it was to get clear of church in Narrowland, even in a place where people waited to leave for someplace else. Just two other travellers that morning. A woman in a green coat sat on the near end of the right front bench, deeply involved in her True Confession. As she turned a page, some ash fell from the cigarette between her fingers and landed on the black patent-leather pocketbook at her side. A little farther down the same bench an old man in overalls and a gray corduroy jacket dozed with his arms crossed on his chest, the brown paper bag next to him giving off the faint smell of potted meat.

Thankful that neither noticed her, Paula chose the opposite bench and sat down at the end farthest away from them. She could see the big clock above the clerk's window: it was eight-thirty; her bus was due to leave at nine. She closed her eyes and pretended to sleep so that the half hour wouldn't turn into a century. But shutting out the clock's face did not stop her remembering eye from scrolling its litany in the darkness behind her lids.

She recognized the images from a dream she'd often had. It begins with a soundless coal train circling a mountain. Naked trees. Brown-gray brush. Each freight car filled with a mound of coal. The locomotive rolls over the rails and vanishes around a curve, and a seemingly endless number of cars follow, so that the mountain appears to be wreathed by a black snake. Black snakes are good for gardens, Paula remembers in the dream. When the caboose finally slips around the bend, the locomotive is already rolling into view again, except that, as it heads for its next disappearance, it shatters what lies before it. The tracks, landscape, all that would be within the scope of an engineer, breaks like a mirror, splintering what Paula thought was there. Then the locomotive disintegrates, too, so that it's hard to tell what is broken "there" and what is shattered train. Now the freight cars follow, but this time the coal is burning, so the fire shatters along with its carriers. As the caboose shivers into pieces, Paula sees that the mountain has changed. Bright green leaves, flame on the trees. Blackberries shine in the brambles. She wonders if she, too, was changed – changed by what she witnessed. Or, by seeing, did she change what she saw? She had yet to dream the dream long enough to find out.

"Nine o'clock's here.

At the sound of the clerk's voice, her eyes snapped open, and in quick, nervous movements, she grabbed the handle of the suitcase and stood up. Not until she had boarded the bus and its wheels were mumbling to the road did she believe that she'd actually managed to get away. Looking out the window, she saw a Yield sign at the head of a side road and thought of yellow jackets, their buried hives. All that hidden sting, waiting to swarm. Perhaps if she opened her mouth, a swarm would spill from her into the rushing past of things beyond the glass. But she kept still; quietly enduring the dogfight of fear, sorrow and giddiness inside her. The dive, buzz, and carom.

She'd been bearing this clamor a long while, when she suddenly remembered the arrowhead, Reaching inside her left coat pocket, she clasped it in her fist. In any other hand, the arrowhead most likely would have been just an interesting piece of flint, but in hers, it was a solace, made of stone that came from the same place as she. And as she held it, she knew it also to be her compass, pointing in only one direction – that of being gone.

We all Fall Down
Joyce Russell

A fox can see well at night, but I can't. I've tried, believe me, I've practiced staring at the side of the barn wall, trying to read the words my brother scratched there years ago. In full daylight they say: 'I hate you all.' But as the sun fades and the last red glow flickers through the trees, they become tall thin scratches: a tally of some sort that was never completed, never struck through.

There should be comfort in darkness because then the words are hidden, but some things don't hide, they lurk, waiting to spring out. And some things don't have to be seen at all: you just always know they are there.

I'd got off the school bus three stops early. Mr Mac, our driver, looked worried.

'Shouldn't you be getting home Kate?' he'd said. 'There's nothing more you can do between here and there.'

He was wrong, of course. There was plenty to do.

Like: watching the sun set, until it looked like the end of a fire left burning on the hill.

Like: dragging my feet through the year's dead leaves, rotting already and turning to slime.

Like: swinging my school bag around me in a circle, just in case it hit any ghosts.

Like: thinking.

Our road is quiet enough. In daylight you can see the old oak trees lining the road and the scattering of holly beneath. There are walls made from rocks piled up high, with earth in between. I know that, because my brother helped repair them once to keep stock in. Really, the wall is just a heap of old sod and stone, but things creep and grow to hold everything together. When my brother pulled the roots out, a whole section fell down.

'Just look at that, Kate,' he said.

I asked him to name the ivy, saxifrage and bindweed that lay pulled around his feet. He did it for me, but I could see it bothered him that something that looked so strong could tumble so quickly.

Maybe I should have stayed on the bus. I could have got off at our gate and walked up to the house. I could have opened the blue painted door and gone in, but it was all too fast. Instead, I'd escaped from Jimmy John popping bubble gum in my ear and Fat Wallace saying: 'leave her alone, because of the day that's in it'.

And I wanted to walk. Even though I hate the dark, and foxes can see in it much better than I can.

There's a sheltered place just ahead, back under the split-trunk tree. It's where the goat died. A big white Billy, with horns that tipped out and back to a point at each end. He had curls in between. Deceptive that! It made you think of little lambs and kiss curls, some sweet kind of innocence. Until you looked in his eyes. They were hard little slits that said: 'If you don't like what I am, then that's tough'.

My Ma said it was because he'd hit into the breeding season and there just wasn't anything around for him to breed with. I don't know about that, but she knows most things.

That white Billy wasn't really white. Close up, he was yellow and had a stink that could place him at a couple of hundred yards. I didn't mind him much. At least I knew when he was coming close and I could hop onto the wall, or up a tree, until he passed by. He took on my Ma though. She chased him back up the road, with a broom waving and her striped pinny flapping. You'd have thought she was a lion tamer, or something. She said she was just defending her own. She didn't want to see her vegetables shredded and her roses nipped. She broke the broom across his back and beat him over the head with the bristle end, but he didn't back down. He kept rearing up on two back legs and dropping those horns down towards her, over and over. My Da had to come and catch him. There's a lot of leverage on horns that big. My Da caught hold and forced them down to the ground. That Billy just had to submit.

They tied him to the tree with a bit of washing line, looping a strong knot so he didn't choke, and that's where he was shot. Three bullets. Or four if you count the one that missed. My Ma had to bath and wash her clothes and my Da had to burn his. The stink just wouldn't come out.

I forgot how fast the night comes in when the days are short. To my right is the hay field. In the summer, it bristles with crackling grass. One time, I whirled around in a circle and plopped down in the centre, hidden, except for the telltale track. I know I shouldn't have flattened the long spikes, but I loved lying silent on my back, watching the clouds slip and slide gently over my green fortress walls.

My brother followed the stepping track, where I'd bent the stalks down. He lifted his feet and placed each one where my foot had fallen. His shoes were bigger, so he blotted out my steps, but he found me all the same. He came upon me so silently, and I was lost in cloud dreams, that I didn't know he was there until he jumped and landed on me, holding my wrists to the ground and laughing with a wide mouth.

We rolled and rolled, flattening more grass. Blotting out the sound of the mowing machine.

My Da pulled us apart. Roaring and spitting in his anger. 'What are you doing?' he demanded. 'Didn't you hear the mower? You could have been cut to pieces!' He struck my brother across the face.

'Don't ever try anything with Kate,' he said.

'You know I'd never do that,' my brother answered and he stared straight into my Da's eyes, until he looked away and started kicking the grass.

This next oak tree is a friend of mine. I think it's safe to stop here for a moment and try to make my breath calm down. I think the tree will protect me from any harm. It has a fork low to the ground, so it's easy to jump up onto a scaly limb. You can walk along the branch, until you are high enough to sit where no one will notice and the fields stretch out around you. It's the best place to have a conversation.

'I don't really mean 'all',' my brother explained. 'When I wrote it, I was angry and I didn't think how the words could hurt. Poor Kate.' He hugged me close, and promised to scratch the 'all' from his words of hate. But I knew it wouldn't work. I was still part of the tally. In some way I didn't understand, I had failed him too.

There's a breeze picking up. I can hear it in the clicking twig fingers above my head. For a moment, it sounds like a car in the distance, heading towards me, but it passes by in the darkness high above. I wonder if it blows ghosts along with it? Swirling up demons from other people's lives and whirling until they land somewhere else, maybe miles away, where no one knows what their moans and groans are all about. But that can't be right: the wind always whips quickly down our valley, and there are still ghosts here. It isn't as easy as to blow them away.

Everything is connected.

Like: Jimmy John saying to Fat Wallace: 'Don't touch her. You might catch something. And your dick will fall off.'

Like: My Da holding onto my brother's arm and hitting him hard around the head as they whirled and whirled in the farm yard.

Like: My mother clutching a magazine to her chest and screaming to stop. Screaming that he can't help it. And when he'd left, she said to me: 'It's just like that old goat, Kate. There's none around here the same kind. He had to go. Better that, than a bullet through the head.'

Like: A magazine that I stole, because I half like it and I half don't understand it.

This is an old backward place, Kate,' my brother said. 'People here would say 'no' to anything that's new. They'd send the best opportunity marching off up the road, just because they don't want to face it. They're afraid that's all. They're afraid of me because I'm different. Don't think badly of me Kate.'

He kissed me gently on the cheek and wiped my tears with his finger.

I begged him to stay, over and over. I twined my fingers in his hair and wouldn't let go, wanting to hold him for ever. I refused to watch when he packed his bag. I shut my eyes when he walked down the road.

I wanted to say that I could never think anything against him. That he'd always been the best brother to me. That if he was different, then I wanted to be different too. If he hated this place, then so did I. I wanted to make a secret pact, but the words wouldn't fall out right, so I said nothing.

There's a taste in the air that's come in on the wind. It's not the tang by the ditch where a fox has marked his run. That only lasts a few paces and then it's gone. This is something cold and elusive, almost metallic. It breathes into the back of my throat and snags a memory. Maybe red at night does mean snow! I have a scarf in my bag, but that means stopping and lifting my arms from the straps. It means dropping the bag to the ground and hunting down among school books and leftover lunch. It might give time for the ghosts to catch up.

'There's no such thing!' my brother laughed. 'Here look.' He flung open the doors of the cupboard on the landing. There were towels and sheets and covers for the spare bed. He pulled out a white cloth and unfurled it like a cloud to drop over his head. We laughed, but it didn't change anything. I always knew that ghosts weren't like that. They live inside of you as much as in the cupboard, or a bend on the road. They slip out as words from under my parent's door:

'He didn't get it from my side of the family.'

'What did we do wrong? We tried didn't we?'

'You shouldn't have hit him so hard is all I'm saying. That won't change anything. Did you see what he wrote on the side of the barn?'

'We were too soft. I should have trashed it out of him years ago. If only I'd known, I could have done something. I'd thought him and Kate. You know. I'd thought they were always together, that something was going on. But I didn't want to see it, so I didn't look too close. Maybe if I had, I'd have seen the truth.'

'He was good to Kate. He always was. From the moment she was born he helped look after her. Did you see her crying when she saw what he'd written? He chased her half way down the road, calling her back.'

Then there was just crying. Ma and Da. Their sobs slipping under the door like formless ghosts.

I can see a light now. It's shining out of the tall window in the gable end. It was by the window that my Dad stopped me. He looked at me sideways, as if he was trying to work something out.

'You don't need to tell people why he left,' he said. 'Just say he's got a job. Gone away to where the money is. Maybe in a year or two, there'll be a wife and child.'

'There won't be!' I said.

He looked at me, through sad eyes.

'And what would you know,' he said. 'Just don't say anything. That's the safest thing.'

So I haven't.

There was no one to talk to anyway. No one to ask what everything meant.

I used to be afraid of our gate by night. I once saw an old crow fly up into the black sky. It made that noise that makes you think it's mocking or knows something you don't. Black and ragged. It faded into the sky too fast. My Da said that crows don't do that. That they don't like the dark any more than I do. He said I was just imagining things. Same as I always do.

My brother said that maybe that old tatty bird just wanted to say hello. That it was prepared to wait around and act a little different, just because it liked me and it wanted to; that eventually it just got too dark and it had to head off. I never found out which one of them was right, but I still look out just in case, as I lift the latch and step through.

There are no birds tonight, but there will be plenty of black and faded suits; people turned out too late to say 'hello'.

The grey stone farmhouse is surrounded by cars. My bedroom is to the far right, with a half window set back in the roof. My brother's room was right next door, so we could tap messages through the wall. I always forgot to knock when I opened his door. That's how I knew. A long time before the rest, I knew. But I never told anyone.

Behind the bright windows, my Ma and Da are moving slowly, polishing glasses and setting them down on the table. Pouring whiskey and sherry; slicing fruitcake. I don't even know if they've missed me yet. Maybe they didn't hear the school bus pass by, or wonder why I hadn't come in with a bang of the door, sliding my school bag across the floor until it hit up against the range.

They are people talking behind the window: neighbours from up and down. I'm tired of being the only one who can't say anything.

Something wet falls on my face. The first soft flakes are tumbling. I stick out my tongue and only close my mouth when I have the act of communion completed.

The warmth of the kitchen is thick around me as I open the door.

Ah Kate, I'm sorry now,' people start to say, as they reach for my hands.

I shrug them off.

'He died of AIDS,' I shout. 'Do you know what that is? My brother was GAY!'

The hands reach out again. 'We know Kate. It's all right, Kate,' they say.

'Someone get her a small drop of whiskey, to calm her down'

'My cousin's brother-in-law was the same way.'

'Sit down, sit down.'

'It's the big city life, that's all.'

'No one blames him, Kate. He was always that way.'

And my Ma: 'You know! Oh my sweet Kate, You know!'

The kitchen lino slides. I tumble down one, two, three.

One: It was everyone's secret, not mine alone.

Two: Why did nobody say?

Three: Because they are protecting me.

And maybe four: That's why he had to leave.

The coffin is laid out in the back room. It's open because Mrs. P from up the road says you don't catch it by sneezing, or looking, or touching a face. There are flowers all around, but I've brought a pocket full of green leaves: a posy full of saxifrage and ivy. I lay my leaves down around his shrunken cheeks. I hold his hand and it's cold and dead, heavy like a lump of clay from a fresh-ploughed field.

I sit for so long that my Ma comes in and blows out the candles that are lit at my brother's head and feet. She puts her arms around me and I feel her muscles squeeze.

'Maybe it's not as dark as you think,' she says. 'You can see all sorts of things if you look hard enough.'

I can't though. I can't see how this lifeless thing is my brother. I can't see why he had come home in a coffin, while we all sang 'ring a rosy' and pretended there was no such thing as the plague. I can't see how being left in the dark helps anything.

'It's the roots that hold everything together,' I say. 'When you pull those out, we all fall down.'

'We did what we thought was best,' my Ma says.

It's snowing hard outside and the wind is picking and blowing a little stronger. It hurls the flakes against ditches and makes rolling waves over the flat fields. I can see by its brightness. There's a drift against the barn wall, covering the words in a layer of pure white.

We'll burry my brother tomorrow, down beneath the earth that grows grass to feed cows, and ivy to twine walls, but can't sustain a rare bloom. For this one night, everything is open, raw and revealed. The truth is possible for a brief moment in time. In a day or two it will be covered back over: Mrs. P. won't use her round mouth to repeat the words AIDS; my Ma won't hold me tight and tell me that I'm not gay just because my brother was. This place will shut its eyes once more against something different walking along the roads, and there won't be anyone for me to ask why a magazine full of naked men is an evil thing. But I won't pretend and I won't forget.

Some ghosts walk step by step at your side, whether you can see them, or not.

The Wake
Alan McMonagle

Now that he was dead and safely buried under the ground well out of harm's way, everyone thought the Briar Martin was a great fellow.

He was full of brains. He had the soul of a poet. He knew everything there was to know about cars. He was a marvellous observer. He was a personal friend of fish.

This upset me no end.

"Why didn't they tell him all this when he was alive and well, making all our lives a misery?" I asked

"Because you can't have your cake and eat it," said my grandfather.

The Briar Martin was my mother's brother, my uncle. He was the black sheep of the family. He never married, never had a career, never had a good thing to say, never smiled – at least not in public. He didn't even own a mobile phone and this signified to everyone that he really wanted nothing to do with the world. His idea of a good time was to rest his elbows on the bar counter, prop his chin in his hands, frown and stare into the black abyss of his glass. He could do this for hours on end. Finally, he might shift in his stool, emit a long grunt, raise his glass and drink deep. His glass was always half full when he ordered another. Or half empty, which everyone assumed was the way he looked at the glass. It was part of his un-cheery outlook, they said. That man was contrary before there were reasons to be contrary, they also said and nodded wisely. Everyone assumed he was an unhappy man.

My mother seemed upset that her brother was dead. But she had another one. One who was married, who had a career, had lots of good things to say and who never stopped smiling – at least not in public. In actual fact, he had two careers, and a car for each of them. He also owned two mobile phones. Which, in a way, made up for the black sheep. His name was Pete.

At the wake for the Briar Martin, Pete spoke to me like a teacher or one of those guys on the radio who always interrupt the songs they play to tell us how good they are. He provided ideas on how to go about tackling the future. Could I rely on my brains, he wondered. Become a solicitor and the owner of a dry cleaning business, he suggested. Don't pay tax at source, he warned. As he spoke, his voice moved up and down and every sentence sounded like it was a question. The first opportunity I got, I ran away from him. Besides, I was interested in finding out more things about the dead man.

Everyone called him the Briar Martin. Including me and my mother and my grandfather. So too, lots of long lost cousins who arrived steadily from New Zealand and Canada and said they couldn't recognise the place. Except Pete. Pete didn't call him anything as his repeated attempts to save his brother from himself had gone unacknowledged. They hadn't spoken together for a long time. But it was a circumstance that affected neither Pete's smiling disposition, nor the Briar Martin's bleak countenance. So perhaps it's true that certain things are best left alone. And also that people don't say what they are thinking.

At the wake, everyone scattered themselves about the room, grabbed sandwiches and talked about the cost of living and climate change. Now and then they considered the dead man's life. They spoke in low huddles but I could hear everything because in those days my mother was keeping me alive with a diet of turnips, and when I tried to tell her they made me feel ill, she placed her hands on her hips and said *eat your turnips or you'll go deaf.* It was something she had to tell me many times. *I can't seem to get through to you* was another thing she often said. So if I wanted to stay alive, let alone not go deaf, I had to eat her lumpy turnips. Otherwise I would perish obscurely like the Briar Martin. It was a difficult choice but, as I chewed the yellow mush, I did notice that my hearing improved remarkably. In fact, though I was still small, I was already at the stage where I could hear the things people were thinking about. So I continued to eat turnips in the hope that I would be able to hear the Briar Martin's opinions on all this royal talk about him – now that he was absent and powerless to disagree.

Because it seemed that everyone was involved in a case of mistaken identity. As far as I could make out, they were talking about a completely different person. I scanned the room to make sure I was attending the correct celebration. I saw my mother, her brother and my grandfather. They were in conversation with people who tripped over themselves to say a great compliment about the dead man – the deceased, they called him. They continued to say only proper and appropriate things. And, concerning my no-good miserable unacknowledging black sheep uncle they even volunteered sympathetic reasons for his anguish.

"Perhaps there was a deep tragedy in his past that prevented him getting on with his life."

"Maybe he was bitter over an unrequited affair of romance."

"His morbidity was down to the unfulfilled promise of youth."

If only he was alive to hear this, I kept saying to myself. He'd set them straight on a few things.

On one thing they were unanimous: He would be missed.

"So why are they saying they miss him?" I asked my grandfather.

"Because it's the truth," he replied.

"But they are telling lies about him. Saying he could fix cars and compose poems and was sensitive like a fish. He was a miserable sod and well they know. They're as bad as my mother."

"What has your mother done to you?"

"She makes me eat turnips. She doesn't even know how to cook them properly. They taste like rocks. Only worse. She says they're good for me and that's a lie."

"If your mother says you must eat turnips, eat them. You'll thank her for it one day."

"I'll thank her on the day I get a decent meal," I said. "A burger and some chips. And onion rings. She is contributing to my distress."

"Don't distress yourself too much, Kevin. Your uncle is at peace."

"So why talk about him like that? Make him out to be a different person?"

"Because there is something worse than talking about someone, no matter what is said," said my grandfather.

"What's that?" I asked.

"Forgetting," he replied.

During this confusing conversation my mother sauntered over. Concerning the progress of her brother's farewell she had probably heard my objections. But I was too worried to notice that she was speaking to me. And then shouting.

"Earth calling Kevin. Come in Kevin. AM I TALKING TO MYSELF?"

She was always saying things like that to me. *Knock, knock. Is there anyone there? Listen carefully; I'm not going to say that again. But she always did and I couldn't stop giggling. That made things between us worse. What does it take to get through to you? I don't know why you were given ears. Are you listening to me Kevin Prendergast?*

She must have had little faith in her turnips, I supposed. Not that I blamed her. But there was not a thing wrong with my ears. It was true I had an alarming pain in the left one when I was very small. I cried and cried and my mother marched me to the doctor and he forced a Hoover inside my head which removed two large waxy black lumps. Then I was given a squirt-bottle of drops and the doctor spoke with my mother. It was shortly after that she started me on the turnips, and my ears announced themselves in the most annoying ways. At night, I could hear water dripping from a faulty tap; the ticking of a distant clock; the pitter-patter of ghosts. Meanwhile, the drops were doing their bit. My ears grew and grew out of the side of my head like aeroplane wings. If I ran fast enough I was sure to take off. If someone took a notion, they could have lifted me up like the winning trophy. So why was my mother so obsessed? If anything, she should have been trying to take my attention away from these freaky growths. And why did she call me by my full name as though I was a complete and utter stranger to her?

All these questions I had no idea how to answer. I returned to my listening and paid attention to three wise-looking men with glasses of whiskey. They were talking but not to each other. They were talking about the Briar Martin and they took turns to say something to the wall they were leaning against.

"He was one of those people with no ambition. No get up and go. No drive. Where I come from, we call those people space-wasters."

"His attitude was wrong. I once heard him mutter when life ends death ends. Life was wasted on him."

"He was born under a pessimistic sign, but I'll say this for him – he was a good man to borrow money off, because he never expected to get it back."

This is more like it, I said to myself. There are still some people who try to tell the truth. These outpourings were much closer to the heart of the matter. It hit me that if everyone was left alone to themselves, really thinking, imagine all the good stuff I could find out. Whiskey was obviously part of it as well.

So I hunted down some lonely people who had turned to drink, and the truly awful things they had to say about the dead man brought an enormous smile to my face. They were mighty things and I hoped they would think similarly of me when my time came. I said as much to my grandfather.

"Somehow, I think things will be different for you," he said. "And you'll outlive us all."

"Oh don't say things like that grandfather," I replied, with a hint of panic in my voice. "It won't be the same with you lot not around to tell lies about me as I pass on to a higher plain."

"Why are you so obsessed with old men and dying?" my grandfather asked me.

"It's the way I am," I replied. "Deep down I am a very troubled person. You could say I am a younger version of the Briar Martin."

"Do you want to be unhappy?" he asked.

"Of course not, but I can't alter my chromosomes."

"Your what?"

"I heard them say that the Briar Martin inherited a bad set of chromosomes. I could have as well."

"And what does your mother think of this chromosome business?"

"Mother definitely has a bad set. She's not able to get through to me. She has started putting rocks in my stew. She says it's for my own good."

My grandfather was laughing now. It was a gentle laugh but it made him sound as if he was out of breath. I thought it was no way to behave on the day of the Briar Martin's wake.

"You don't know what it's like grandfather," I pleaded. "Some of my troubles go so deep a submarine wouldn't find them."

But my yearning fell on another pair of deaf ears. He was also bending over and his face was reddening from all laughter. A ropey vein throbbed out of his neck and blue wriggly strands appeared on his nose.

"This isn't a laughing matter, grandfather," I said as sternly as possible.

"No, no it isn't. But you shouldn't take things to heart so much."

That was the last straw. As far as I was concerned. I was now in official dispute with everyone close to me. My rock-baking mother. Her career-collecting brother. And now my laughing grandfather. None of these people seemed prepared to take my anxieties seriously. What was the point in being alive if you couldn't take things to heart? I had to get this through to them and I saw only one other course of action left to me to take.

Just before the fiddle players started pulling their bows of woe and regret. I announced my intentions to go on hunger strike.

And I went outside.

I sat on the garden wall, rested my chin in my hands and tried to frown the way I had seen the Briar Martin do it on one of the last times I had seen him. It was during an especially difficult time for my mother to get through to me. I couldn't bear to listen to anything she tried to say to me and one afternoon I escaped from the house and followed the Briar Martin into the pub. It was my first time in the pub. It was small and narrow, with a low ceiling and no windows. My uncle was the only other person there. He recognised me and he gestured to a stool beside him. He put a mineral in front of me and it was quiet for a long time. The two of us just sat there and I enjoyed the silence. "Do you know why I like this place so much?" he said to me after an age. "There is no coverage for mobile phones." Then he chuckled away to himself.

Eventually, my mother tried to tease me out of my strike. She came to me with a bowl of mush and I told her what I thought of her cooking. Her brother appeared with his up and down voice and I added not-talking to my strike. Then they sent out my grandfather.

He sat down on a low wall and didn't say a thing. I soon became fed up with all this quiet between us.

"Are you not talking either?" I asked him.

"It seems you and I have something in common," he said. "When I was in the army they fed us turnips. It was during The Emergency. Don't ask me about the Emergency because I haven't got all day to put you in a good mood. But you're right about one thing. I have just tasted your mother's cooking. These turnips need something."

Later, after everyone had eaten all the sandwiches and drank the whiskey and wobbled off to stare longingly at the Briar Martin's empty bar stool, grandfather showed us how to make an onion gravy that soaked up every single piece of turnip on the plate. Straightaway they tasted better and that night I heard the dead whispering jokes to each other.

In years to come, many more unhappy uncles and aunts came out of the woodwork to be buried. I returned from my own quest for happiness and spent a few days with my mother and my uncle Pete who, by then, had accumulated four careers, five cars, a cottage on the island of Cyprus, a valuable portfolio of mobile phones and three spoilt brats via a second wife. It's best not to mention his voice.

And I developed a genuine liking for turnips, a development which has aided beyond measure my joust with life, as I can hear what people are saying in Africa and Ecuador and I listen to what everyone thinks and I know parts of the answers to questions before I even ask them. So no one is fooling me.

I even rang my mother and thanked her – just like grandfather said I would. I could hear him laughing as well, wherever he was, and his gentle wheezing reminded me of youthful time spent in his company searching for the roots of my unhappiness. Unforgotten time. And it occurs to me that maybe I hadn't been as troubled as I thought I was.

If Our God Is God What's Their God?

Toby McGrath

The meals are as bad as they are cheap in this place but it doesn't bother Tony Monroe. It bothers his lunch date Marion Kearny. She stabs a piece of lifeless lettuce with her fork and holds it up for inspection.

"Why do you eat here Tony?"

"It's cheap."

She drops the dead vegetation onto her plate.

"Tony, I'm going to head back. I need to clear up a few things before the meeting."

Tony grunts goodbye on account of his mouth being fully engaged in an awesome demolition of an elastic lasagne.

Back in the office Marion's page-a-day desk calendar shows yesterday's date. Before she tears off the bold black seven, she reads the small red rubric written beneath it. This is a recent habit. The little message says freedom flows from moral certainty. She balls it and tosses it into the bin. Her only thought is that the next time the number seven makes a solo appearance, Marion Kearney will be three decades mooching around on planet Earth.

The single entry in her diary for the afternoon of Friday the eighth is the obligatory end of week meeting. It doesn't take long to pull the relevant files and paste her report together. When it's done she phones her folks to let them know she'll be down for the weekend. It's been a while since they moved out of town and her visits have been sporadic at best. As she listens now to her mam and dad enthuse about early springtime in the countryside, a thought that she might be pregnant disturbs her. When the call ends she leans back in her chair, does a quick mental tally, and knows it's not possible. Knows it's possible but more than highly improbable. It might explain her current listlessness, but then so might the weather.

The meeting lasts an hour and an hour has never dragged so slowly. Luckily for Marion her projects are either in production or at a stage of development where she isn't expected to say much. After a brief and perfunctory report she spends the afternoon listening and nodding and drifting. It's her lunch date Tony Monroe who gets to do most of the talking. The company is working hard to secure a new beer commercial and it's Tony's baby. He gives an upbeat assessment of how things are progressing. Tony is good on facts and figures, costs and cost-cutting. Marion can personally vouch for his cost-cutting talent. When she finds herself wondering if it's a trick of the light or is that a shiny grease blob on Tony's chin, she knows she needs this meeting to end soon. Tony obliges by wrapping up his report which is followed by some questions, answers, and suggestions. The meeting breaks up and as she turns to go Marion is tapped on the shoulder.

"Ms. Kearney… are you a little under the weather?"

"No more than usual Brian. Why do you ask?"

"I thought you were somewhat distracted there. But okay then, you're fine. So tell me, any plans for the weekend?"

Brian Broughan is the owner of the company. Brian's a committed family man and a dedicated sailor who spends most of his winter weekends readying his boat for the coming season.

"I told the folks I'd visit them in their rustic retreat. How about you?"

"Oh you know me Marion, the usual. And the good news is, she's nearly ready for the high seas. You're coming to see her?"

"I am Brian."

"You always says that Ms. Kearney but you never do. I'm going to have to pin you down one of these days."

Coming from one or two of the others in the office there'd have been heavy innuendo attached to that, but not with Brian.

"Mr. Broughan, just as soon as it's a barge fit for a princess…"

"Whoa now… none of that barge business please. But you've got yourself a deal."

He gives her a thumbs up and leaves the office. Gerry Gibson tugs her sleeve.

"Hey Kearney… you comin' across to Grogans with us? It's Breda's last drink on account of… you know."

"Love to Gerry, but I'm heading out of town. You guys have one for me."

Back in her office Marion files away the report, puts on her jacket and grabs her bag.

"What's this I hear about you not coming to Grogans?"

Breda Kane is standing in the open doorway. She's all of two months pregnant and she's calling a halt to beer and cigarettes for the duration.

"I'd love to Breda, but I'm on a promise to visit the folks."

"Ah come on Marion, I'm having just the one myself. Then it's Blessed Breda until I drop the sprog. Anyhow, you'd be off your rocker to head out into the Friday madness now."

"I'll go for one Breda, just the one."

Breda is true to her word and leaves after one drink. Marion is on her fifth when she tangles awkwardly with a high stool and comes down heavily on her ankle. Something might have cracked, she isn't sure, but it hurts. When the ankle balloons they put her in a taxi for the hospital.

In the muggy warmth of the waiting room Marion's head sags. For a Friday night the crowd isn't so big and she persuades herself it won't take too long. A painful throb radiates along her leg. Her droopy eyes hide from the fluorescent glare and she sinks into her plastic chair.

"It's early yet. Third World conditions don't set in till later. At closing time…"

She turns her head to identify the speaker. He's a number of seats away on her right. There's nobody between them. Two intense eyes lock onto her when he speaks again.

"Did they ask you what religion are you?"

He's sixty or seventy, rumpled-skinned and skinny inside a suit equally rumpled and at least one size too big. An unexpectedly white and shiny pate is at dramatic variance with a heavy five o'clock shadow. A flat cap revolves slowly between his fingers. Marion is not in the mood.

"I'm here to see a doctor."

"Oh! Sorry for the impertinence."

Before she looks away the man speaks again.

"But it makes you think all the same, doesn't it?"

"Listen, I'm not into small talk at the minute."

"I can see that. It's written in large script all over your face."

Marion couldn't be less bothered what the old fart sees inscribed on her face, so long as he leaves her alone. She turns away just as he speaks again.

"Doubt does it. It's everywhere. It must be free with cornflakes."

Marion's been round the block enough times to know when to fully disengage, and a quick glance tells her to fully disengage post-haste. Mr Rumpledsuitskin's two goggle eyes are up for something, and whatever it is, it's not for her. She's tired and in pain. She wants to see a doctor and go home. In a blatantly theatrical manoeuvre, she faces forward, folds her arms, lowers her head, and closes her eyes. The old guy says something Marion purposely doesn't catch and she makes no response, but from somewhere to her left the bait is taken.

"That's me all over. Never certain of a thing."

It's a woman's voice. Marion keeps her head down. Let the pair of them at it. The woman speaks again.

"And where did it get me?"

"That's it."

"Never reached me proper potential."

The goggle eyed inquisitor waits a decent two seconds before he fires the question.

"Did you tell them a religion?"

"I did."

The woman leaves it at that and Marion knows the old codger is bursting a gut. How long can he leave it hanging? As the silence lengthens she has to bury her face in her hands, because if they see her laughing she'll be dragged into the fray. He doesn't leave it long hanging.

"You don't have to give them a religion."

"It's on the form."

"But you don't have to say!"

"I didn't mind. I said if I was anything I was probably a Christian."

"Ah no, you can't be a Christian."

"Why can't ye?"

"Not anymore."

"Why can't ye?"

"Not a religious one anyhow."

"Are you goin' to tell me why can't ye?"

"If you're a Christian, doesn't that infringe on the rights of the others?"

"What others?"

"Whoever isn't a Christian! Jews and Muslims… even pagans."

"How does it do that?"

"Maybe even atheists."

"How does it do that?"

"If you say your god is god, then what's their god?"

This is like fucking pantomime. This is why A&E sells out every Friday night. Maybe a rabbi or a mufti will come in for repairs and take it to a whole new level. If it weren't for the pain, Marion has no doubt she'd enjoy the show. It's better than the pub. But she's too sore. She'll have to get hold of a nurse. Every now and then an apparition in white zips passed on some sort of high energy batteries.

"Excuse me… nurse… hello!"

"Just a minute…"

"Nurse, I just want to…"

But the vision is gone. Marion feels bad badgering the staff but she's still waiting in the triage queue to get into the doctor queue. She stands on her good foot and gingerly puts the bad one on the floor. She hobbles a couple of painful steps before a voice stops her.

"You should stay off that foot until…"

"Listen, nurse, is there something you could give me, to get me home? I don't think this is bad enough to waste your time."

"You should let us…"

"I'll come back tomorrow, but could you give me something, to get me home? Please?"

"That's not the way it works I'm afraid."

"No, that'd be too easy. So I get back in the queue for the queue? No thanks!"

Before she manages to limp her way to the exit doors, the angel of mercy has brought two capsules and a plastic cup of water.

"Swallow this. It's anti-inflammatory and it'll do something for the pain. This one's for later."

In the taxi to her flat she phones her folks to say the weekend visit is off. She manages to tell them about the ankle without mentioning the pub. They wonder how she'll manage on her own over the weekend, and her mam can't help mentioning the piper. Marion says it's not so bad she can't cope for a couple of days. She concedes she might see the piper this weekend, but it's not likely.

"We're not an item anymore mam, I told you. We're friends, that's it."

When she ends the call she's thinking about the piper. He's still a good pal. A good pal is what you need when you need some comfort. Maybe he'll be in one of his usual Friday night haunts. She asks the driver.

"Do you know the Pipers' Club, near the Motor Tax office?"

"Ah no love, the Pipers' is in Henrietta Place."

"Oh yeah..."

"I'll bet you're thinking of..."

"Yeah, no it's not the Club... but there's a session in... you know the place, just off the quays, beside the Motor Tax office..."

She winces her way from the taxi to the little cloud of banned smokers huddled outside the door of the pub, and licit and illicit weed odours trail after her as she hobbles inside.

"Marion Kearney, are you on or off the wagon or what?"

Even as she explains about having to get her arse onto the seat because of the foot, Bill Dawson has her drink included in a round. The session is swinging and she squeezes in beside a couple of half familiar faces. Lennie the piper is at the far side of the circle of musicians.

There's no talking while the players play and Marion watches Lennie, his eyes creased closed in hard concentration. This man can coax a mean tune from wood and leather when he wants to. The last time they were properly together he was doing another type of coaxing. He asked how long she intended drifting. She asked what business was it of his. He said it probably wasn't any, and they didn't fight, and from then on they didn't do much of anything except slowly drift apart.

The set ends and Lennie sees her and friendly nods are exchanged. She watches him take his raggedy chamois and wipe the chanter. The same chamois she bought him. She remembers the time her mam said the piper wouldn't be a bad catch. And he wouldn't, if you were to look at things that way. But then a girl would have to be in the mood for catching, and for getting caught, and a piper in the mood for getting caught and… ah shit, it's too complicated.

"Bottoms up Bill Dawson!"

"Sláinte go deo Marion Kearney!"

A lazy lyrical lament arrives with perfect timing because at last the pain pill is doing its job. Marion lets herself go with the crying pipes and a sleepy warm mellowness seeps through her. She melds with the melody until the achingly beautiful slow air tries to take her to a place she's not ready to be taken. She breaks the spell and signals for another round. Same again.

At the end of the session a slim tight-haired girlie-woman carries two drinks across to Lennie and helps him pack away his pipes. That's my job is Marion's immediate impulse. Lennie leans down and kisses the trim thing. It's a brief brushing of lips but it's clear she's not his sister. Ah shit. Shit shit shit!

"Hey, isn't this what it's all about Marion Kearney?"

"What else could it be about Bill Dawson?"

"Enjoying the music and having the craic."

"If it was about anything else Bill, we'd be in trouble."

"Big trouble Marion. Big trouble."

"Sláinte!"

Explosions
James Harkin

The first time I seen anything explode, it was the man next door. I'm not saying he went up in flames exactly, but by the time the ambulance arrived in a vain attempt to put Sammy Johnson back together again, he'd probably shed a few stone. That's the funny thing about a small bomb hurled directly in the direction of a man. There's not much blood or anything like that, it's not like getting shot or torn apart limb from limb like they do on the TV. No, Sammy Johnson was still in one piece – two or three pieces, maximum. It's just that what remained of him looked as if it had been grilled, neatly and lovingly barbecued beyond all recognition and then laid out in miniature for everyone to admire.

The best way to put it is that Sammy Johnson was burnt to adams. That was the phrase the policeman used, the one who came and sat beside me on the bed and wrote down everything I told him. "Poor Sammy", he said, shaking his head – "burnt to adams". He repeated the phrase so many times I'm sure he must have wrote it down in the little black book he took out of his breast pocket. He was certainly writing something down because he kept scribbling and turning over pages by licking them with his finger. If the policeman was sitting beside me on my bed, it's because he was a friend of both my Da's and Sammy Johnson's – they'd served together – and had met me many times before. And if he needed to sit down on the end of my bed, that was because Sammy Johnson, like my Da and the policeman, used to be part-time member of the Royal Ulster Constabulary, the central fact which explained why – in the words of the policeman who sat on the end, out of puff and performing acts of logical arithmetic worthy of Sherlock Holmes – he was now tatty bread. Meaning dead, meaning RIP, meaning no more free Mars bars and Cokes from poor old Sammy. And if he, this overweight, sweating meathead of a policemen, sat and hugged me so tight I nearly choked and cried uncontrollably into my sweater, maybe he was trying to counsel me in addition to taking my witness statement. Maybe he was only trying to be there for me, to forge an emotional bond with the young Michael Lavery – a Catholic, to boot, but a decent one – which might help him to process emotionally what he had just witnessed. Those were the days before they had therapists, of course, and certainly before they had policewomen who pretended to be therapists and told you to write it all down just so they'd get everything out of you.

I was thirteen years old when Sammy went up in smoke. The funny thing was, you'd think that we – me, everyone and especially Sammy – should have seen it coming. Nearly a year before Sammy got burnt to adams, he was out in his front garden picking out weeds when a van screeched around the corner of our street and three men in balaclavas got out. I wasn't there – I was at school – but the way Sammy told it afterwards they raced towards him and threw a bomb right into the garden where he was working. Thinking on his feet, Sammy had picked up his spade and – in the manner of an Olympic shot-putter – hurled the makeshift bomb right back into the road where it promptly exploded. The balaclavas retreated back to the van and screeched back from where they came and that was that. For months afterwards, Sammy was leaning over his garden fence and telling everyone who'd listen about his lucky escape, about how he got one over on the "bad bastards" with the help of his trusty green fingers. "Bad boys", he used to say, and then shake his head – as if that was the sum total of his criteria for moral judgement, that the world could be divided, like a classroom, into good boys and bad. Sammy and his spade had their picture taken in the local paper. He even won one of those medals they give out and spent the day outside Belfast at some ceremonial where they pinned it to his chest. Apart from that, the only evidence of any disturbance was a crater in the road which those slovenly townies at Belfast City Council took months to get around to filling in.

What stoic Sammy didn't understand until his dying day was the adaptability of life and the people in it to signals within their immediate environment. About eight months after he threw the bomb back in the faces of his attackers, he was working in the garden again on a Saturday afternoon when another van screeched around the corner and three men in balaclavas jumped out. For all I know, they might have been the same ones. One of them raced towards him and threw another makeshift bomb into Sammy's garden. By all accounts, Sammy raced towards it and tried to perform the same trick again. This time, however, the balaclavas had had the foresight to make the bomb touch-sensitive – a cunning modification of the initial attack as a direct consequence of which Sammy exploded. Dressed in my first communion blazer and a black and red tie, I accompanied my mother and father to the funeral in a Protestant Church. Nobody was crying but Mrs Johnson fainted. At the wake afterwards, swarms of hulking, awkwardly dressed old men stood around like bottles of stout, eating limp white sandwiches and drinking pints of Guinness, all of them shaking their heads and saying that the people who could do that to Sammy "must be bad boys". What I still can't work out was why they didn't just shoot him in the first place, like civilised gunmen, instead of throwing a bomb at him. Maybe it was some kind of code of honour, the determination to give him a sporting chance by entering him involuntarily for a Northern Irish (version?) of the shot-putt. Or maybe it was some kind of macabre ritual designed to test out a new kind of bomb, like the ones I heard they used to hurl almost randomly over the walls of the police stations as if for luck. At the funeral there were murmurs that it wasn't the IRA at all but a splinter group. "They'll lift the boys who did it soon enough", someone said. "Hanging isn't good enough for them", replied another. But all that came too late for Sammy, who was tatty bread.

The truth is, however, that the balaclavas were not the only bad boys on the day when Sammy was picked up and put in the back of an ambulance. Not only was I upstairs at the time of Sammy's second encounter with the balaclavas but I wasn't, to tell you the God's honest truth, looking out my bedroom window at Sammy's front garden at all. If I pretended I was when the policeman came in and sat down with his notebook, that was only because in all the commotion I honestly began to think that I had been. But that wasn't the only reason for my little white lie. The truth was that I pretended to be at the bedroom window staring down at Sammy because the alternative was not going to look good when written down in that policeman's notebook, not one tiny wee bit. Saturday, you see, was the day that my Ma and Da had gone out to the shops, leaving yours truly to mind the house. As soon as I heard the distinctive rumble of my Da's diesel disappear up the street, I raced, as I did every Saturday back then, down the stairs into a pokey basement where he kept everything from his chamois leathers for washing the car to his Black and Decker power drill.

Now I wasn't a great man for tools or machines – I still amn't – but I was madly in love with a certain red and black vacuum cleaner which my Da kept in a cubby hole under the stairs. As soon as I'd get the place to myself – which was very whackabout, since my Da was always doing police and my Ma was busy at the teaching – I'd race down the stairs, grab the vacuum cleaner from out of its cubbyhole, plug it into the wall, sit down on a chair, drop my trousers and whack myself off in the most unusual way. I'd switch the cleaner on by pressing down the knob on the top at the mains and tentatively – you've got to do this tentatively, if you want to avoid doing yourself an injury – take out my dick and stick it right into the vacuum cleaner pipe. It takes some practice, and at the beginning you've got to take things very slow, but the experience is nothing short of phenomenal. Sometimes I'd bring a nudie magazine or two and set them down on the floor to read while I did it; occasionally I'd even dress up in one of my mum's tweed skirts, put on a pair of her tights and make an afternoon of it. One time I even rang one of those telephone sex lines where you talk to one of the operators and she pretends to be wearing lingerie and panting and everything – the ones you see in the paper, where it says you can talk about anything you want. But the one time I called, the woman complained about the noise and hung up.

I spent some of my happiest moments of my adolescence in the company of that vacuum cleaner, playing it like a set of bagpipes, embracing it with both hands outstretched as if in an invitation to dance, revving it up and down by playing with the knob until I lost patience and decided it was ready to come. It was short and squat, if I remember rightly, and one thing I'll never forget is that it had been branded with a pair of quizzical eyes and a smiley face painted on its side. I lost my virginity to that hoover; I still maintain it was one of the best lovers I ever had. The only problem was that my furtive liaisons with it were always cut short, circumscribed by the limited time I had before my parents came home. In any other circumstances there would have been no problem in knowing when they'd arrive home – the distinctive grumble of a Diesel engine was enough to give that away – but vacuum cleaners make a terrible racket, and the racket you get putting my dick in the pipe of one, a noise somewhere between a loud billowing and a merciless self-battering, is nothing short of deafening. I had, in short, to remain alert and to keep my ears open all the time. Even if I did hear the car from up the road, that still only left me about three minutes to put back on my clothes and put back my mum's clothes where they belonged, thoroughly clean the inside of the vacuum cleaner pipe of sexual residue, put it back where it belonged, and get back to my bedroom and sit pretending to read a copy of "Commando". The result was that my very first orgasms arrived on a knife-edge of tension, balanced on a fulcrum with one eye on the door-handle and one ear on the road outside.

Imagine how I felt, then, when this loving synthesis of man and machine was interrupted by Sammy's exploding into thin air? I'd been sitting there for all of a few minutes, delicately playing a range of notes and vibrating hums on the cleaner, carefully bringing myself to a peak of sexual intensity with the aid of that noisily powerful sucking machine while at the same time coolly listening out for the signal that these few stolen moments were going to have to come to a hasty end. The first I heard of Sammy's departure from the mortal world was a dull thud of a bang, which, given the delicately-wrought circumstances in which my body was arranged, was not quite enough to short-circuit the sudden, painful suction of my ejaculate into the pipe but was more than enough to give me one of the frights of my life. Jesus Christ, I remember thinking, Jesus Christ. It was so loud and so quick that for that for a moment I considered the possibility that my mute convulsions and my viscous ejaculate had forced the vacuum cleaner into some kind of electrical malfunction, that it had fused everything in the local area with a giant firecracker of a bang and that it was very shortly going to take my genitals with it. All I was thinking, as I raced up the stairs and over to my bedroom window, was that something terrible had gone wrong and that now the police would be coming – and wondering how long they would take, whether they'd arrive before I'd cleaned up my mess, and what kind of unlikely excuse I could make up if I hadn't.

So the truth is that I never did see the explosion at all, wrapped up as I was in my own little private explosion and its aftermath. But there was, I think, one final reason why I pretended to have borne witness to Sammy's last afternoon in his garden. The way I see it now, I think I pretended I'd heard the explosion because I was desperate to play a part in all that excitement, and couldn't bear the idea that I'd been so close to it but yet so far away. Everyone would be talking about it for months afterwards, in the same way that they'd talked about Sammy's previous encounter with the bombers, and it would really add something if I pretended that I saw it, that I was everyone's intrepid man on the ground. In a way, it was the least I could do for old Sammy – after all those Mars bars and Cokes – to pretend to bear witness to his final moments. He wouldn't, after all, be around to brag about this time. Back then, you see, it was as if the whole Christian calendar was punctuated with holy days and major explosions – you'd talk about them endlessly, people would shake their heads piously or wail or appear on TV saying that the people who did this must be mad, must be animals, must be not right in the head. Or loop the loop; one time me and a friend from school doubled up laughing when we heard a mother on the evening news say that the people who killed her husband must be loop the loop, coincidentally the name of a popular Northern Ireland ice cream in those days, put together out of sugary strips of green, yellow and white, and which the size of the oul' doll being interviewed suggested she was no stranger to at all. In the event of a major explosion or an all-out riot in which the buses couldn't get through, sometimes you wouldn't even have to go to school.

The thing was, I was beginning to welcome explosions of all kinds – bombings, shootings, hijacking and riots – and even to look forward to them, because they brought everyone together in a fit of excitement, and made the dull business of going to school in a glum, grey little province like Northern Ireland a great deal more palatable. It wasn't so much the attacks themselves I enjoyed – get caught up in one of those and you could easily wind up, like Sammy, in plastic bags – but the aftermath, the whispering in ominous tones, the news coverage which interrupted the snooker or the football on television, the extended post mortem in jokes and conversations at school which lasted for weeks afterwards, or at least until the next bomb went off.

If you're looking for one reason above all else why I did what I did, why I became what I later became, it's because I'd come to think that the odd explosion, or fear of an explosion, is probably good for people. It shakes things up and gets people talking. You out of all people ought to be in favour of that.

Daddy Dead

Julia Van Middlesworth

You can buy baby pigs feet in a jar. I know – Aunt Oink buys them at A&P and makes me eat them. They're pink as ballerina slippers and my baby sister. The toes point toward the bottom of the jar. Aunt Oink doesn't care that the pigs were babies; she eats them just the same. I watch her chew and swallow to make sure she doesn't spit them out. The vinegar burns my nose and I feel bad for the pigs. They didn't ask to be born. I heard Auntie Oink say that the meat is tender but I can't chew it and it sticks in my throat. I wonder if they kill the piglets before they chop off their feet. Maybe there is a farm of piglets without feet somewhere in Nebraska. I shake the jar and watch the feet bob inside the glass – they look as if they're trying to run away. The next time Aunt Oink and Daddy Dead force me to eat a pickled pig's knuckle they'll be sorry. Today we found the key.

Mother Blind goes shopping and Aunt Oink baby-sits for my brother and sister and me. Daddy Dead and Aunt Oink play games while Mother Blind buys Wheaties and Popsicles. He grabs her boobs and she squeals. Mother Blind can't see but Knife and I do. I try to tell her but she won't listen.

Knife is my Barbie doll. We invent names for everyone – our secret code. I renamed Barbie "Knife" because she dresses sharp and protects me like a knife. My mother's real name is Jane but we call her Mother Blind. She always says: "Hear no evil, see no evil, speak no evil." How do you do that? Die? There's a picture of three monkeys over the kitchen stove as a reminder – one with paws covering his eyes; the middle monkey's paws pressed over his mouth and the third monkey's paws placed on his ears.

I'm eight-years-old. Most nights when Aunt Oink baby-sits, Daddy Dead comes home early and they drink beer and smooch. Daddy Dead smells like Old Spice Cologne and whiskey. His hair is the color of rust and combed in a wave over his forehead. By the time my mother gets home his hair is on end and his words slide together.

He catches me staring at him and says: "What-you-looking-at?"

Daddy's teeth point and there's so many it makes me afraid when he smiles. But sometimes he's handsome and he always drives a new Buick and takes me for rides. I wait in the car while he stops at a bar called The Elbow. Once he let me come in with him and he bought me a ham sandwich. Bonnie who works the bar makes them four inches high with ham. I can't finish when I remember the pig's feet but I eat the potato chips and the whole pickle. When I asked Mommy where the meat comes from she said from animals

"How can that be?"

"They kill them."

"No!"

"It's true."

I couldn't believe it. All this time I've been eating babies and mothers and fathers! Mr. Murray's farm has cows and they lick salt from my hands. Cleo has a black velvet spot over one eye.

Aunt Oink's real name is Margaret Alice but people call her Allie for short. Whenever she wiggles into a room I smell her perfume. She dabs it behind her ears and on her wrists from a midnight blue bottle called Evening In Paris. It reeks. I know that Paris doesn't smell that way. Paris is full of candlelight and ballerinas and probably smells like fresh baked bread all the time – nothing like Aunt Oink's putrid perfume.

I read about Paris France in the travel section of the bookstore where Aunt Oink goes to buy her astrology magazines. Paris has the Seine River that lights up at night with stars like the Hayden Planetarium at the Museum of Natural History. I went there on a class trip with Mr. Zagoria. When they turn out the lights you look up and the ceiling is like a giant upside-down teacup filled with stars. It makes you feel as if you're spinning through the galaxy like a feather not knowing where you'll end up.

Sometimes Aunt Oink snorts from the horoscope section and I duck behind the bookshelves and slink far behind her when she struts out the door.

Once, I called her Aunt Snort when she laughed and afterwards, she chased me with dagger-red fingernails that left red half moons up and down my arms. I squeezed the crescent moons to bleed out all the poison. I carry bad blood from my father. My mother told me this.

My Daddy's name is Henry J. Sometimes we call him Daddy Belt but mostly we call him Daddy Dead. He holds a pillow over my face. Daddy likes to tease me with a pillow. I can't scream in the pillow because I can't breathe so I repeat the words Daddy Dead over and over so I won't die. As long as I can repeat the words I know I'm alive. The pillow smells of chicken feathers and I go to the sleepy place and learn to leave my body. The inside part of me rises up to the ceiling – I look down on Aunt Oink and Daddy Dead pressing the pillow over my face. Maybe this is what they mean by "go to heaven". Maybe this is what they mean by "God."

When my eyes open Daddy glares down at me, he grins and a whiff of whiskey blows in my face. He drinks the whiskey with Jesus on the label. I see all Daddy's teeth, molars and incisors, square ones and pointy ones. One time I bit his hand but then he was Daddy Belt. Aunt Oink enjoys it when I get the belt. Her lips part brick-red and her eyes shoot black nails at me. Daddy Dead's belt makes a hissing sound before it cracks my skin.

"Some day you'll learn. Children should be seen and not heard," he says.

Mother Blind turns away. She doesn't like ugly things. They give her a heart attack. She cares for babies and fries chicken all day. My baby sister splashes in the kitchen sink. She kicks her feet in the suds as if she's running away. My mother scrubs and scrubs babies and floors till the bubbles collapse. She hates dirt.

“Cleanliness is next to Godliness,” she says, as she rolls a chicken leg in a hill of flour. Flour clouds rise around her head and make the kitchen foggy. Maybe that’s why she can’t see. Probably her eyes absorbed the flour and made her blind. Knife and I watch the yellow legs and wings – the plump breasts sizzle in the pan. Where do all the feathers go? I imagine they drift to the sky and stuff the clouds. Sometimes Mother Blind tucks the chicken wings in a roasting pan. They lay sideways like the arms of unborn babies. I wonder if the chickens and pigs have a way to cry.

I used to cry but now I’m a soldier – my tears go inside instead of out. Daddy Dead taught me how. If I cry I get the belt, he doesn’t like when I slobber. Knife says I better slice my food so the tears can drain out in a bucket. That way I can dump them down the toilet. If that doesn’t work I might drown – there’s probably tadpoles swimming up and down inside my legs.

At night Mother Blind reads my brother the story of “The Three Little Pigs” and he huffs and puffs and tries to blow our house down.

Some nights I dream about Mr. Wolf. He wears a cap and a suit jacket and does a jig up our walk crossing his legs with a little jump while holding his tail up like the train of an evening gown. He leans down over my bed and whispers in my ear: *Blow-**Dooooooooooown**-your-house*. The words stretch like chewing gum, then he laughs and skips back up the walkway and into the forest.

We found the key in Aunt Oink’s bible. Knife has a locator-eye.

It has a black leather cover with gold letters. We found The Bible buried in Aunt Oink’s red underwear. I flip the pages and smell Evening in Paris perfume. The words in The Bible scare me. Knife holds her arms straight like a zombie and her hair stands on end in pikes. Our reflections jump out from Aunt Oink’s mirror and we almost, but don’t scream. The gold key peeks out from the shadow of death.

A large brassiere hangs from a hook in the corner like a giant muzzle. Aunt Oink’s boobs are everywhere like the universe. She wears tight sweaters that she takes off when my Daddy Dead clicks her photo. I see them through the crack in my bedroom door. Purple and black spots pop in my eyeballs and my stomach feels full of pig’s feet. Daddy has a darkroom and the photos are born in smelly washtub.

Everything was better before she grew boobs. Daddy played guitar and sang me: "Hey Good Lookin' What Ya' Got Cookin'?" Sometimes Mommy sang, "Stormy Weather." Then they kissed.

I keep the key in the bottom of my shoe. It feels cool and solid as a quarter and rubs against my sock. I curl my toes around the fancy edges. Now we just have to find the jewellery box. Knife and I spy from the crack in the door but Aunt Oink turns and we have to run before she hides it. Knife suspects it's in the closet and she's always right. Her left eye spins blue then green when the special radar picks up a location.

I like to sew Knife clothes and accessories.

"You're possessed by The Devil!" Aunt Oink tells me. "A big fat devil with red horns, a black pitch fork and flames for eyes! You're going to Hell! You'll burn for eternity. The Devil will put you in a boiling pot of water but you will ***never*** die!"

All because I cut up one of her bras to make Knife a parachute.

Knife used to have boobs but I performed surgery and buried them in the backyard by King Car. I hope I never grow evil boobs. Aunt Allie used to buy me Almond Joy and Mars bars. Once we tried to fry an egg on the hot sidewalk and she showed me a photograph of nude tribesmen and we giggled.

King Car is our hideout – a junky Dodge. If you saw King Car you'd think of a rusted tuna fish can with jelly jar windows and wheels flat as sardines. King Car rots in the backyard partly hidden in a tangle of bushes – thorny ones that pierce my legs right through my jeans and fluffy ones too, with plumes that whirl in the air when I crack open the car door. Knife and I see King Car from the kitchen window and dream of the places we'll go. King Car starts when I'm at the wheel. We go to important cities like New York and even Paris – places without chicken or pig farms.

Before we go to sleep we dream of all the lights in Paris to stop thinking about the clouds over the roof and how they might press down like pillows and smother us. Today we found the jewellery box buried in the hamper in Aunt Oink's closet. Knife is always right but before we could unlock it, high heels click down the hall and we slip out of the door in the nick of time.

We'll have to wait until she's sleeping; snorting in her pillow.

Mother Blind knots her black scarf. She's driving to the grocery store. First she checks her face in the mirror and twists her mouth into an odd shape when she studies her reflection. Maybe she doesn't want to recognize herself because she doesn't sing "Stormy Weather" anymore. Her brown coat has a fur collar that curls around her neck. I said it looked like a monkey tail and she told me I have a dirty mouth.

Mother Blind turns from the mirror to Aunt Oink and says: "Is my lipstick on straight? I'll pick up a loin roast for tomorrow night. I found a new recipe in Woman's Day."

Aunt Oink just shrugs her shoulders. She's filing her nails at the kitchen table.

"I shouldn't be too long." She looks at my brother and me and says:

"Now don't let me find a filthy pig pen when I get back."

I want to tell her she should tell Aunt Oink but she slams the door shut.

Aunt Oink chomps on a headcheese sandwich in between filing her nails. She bites the white bread and leaves two red slashes. If she knew about the key she'd be mad. Even if she calls a firing squad I won't give it up. Next time Daddy Dead and Aunt Oink force me to eat a pig's foot I'll give them what they deserve.

Someday Aunt Oink will be old and I'll make her eat her own fingers and toes.

I cut Knife a black jumpsuit out of Daddy Dead's black leather gloves and take the army helmet and machine gun from my brother's G.I. Joe. Now she's a soldier. I snip her hair so it stands in spikes like a hand grenade. It was Knife's idea to put the photographs in the oven.

We spy Aunt Oink from our room. She finishes her sandwich, lights a cigarette and opens a beer. She's reading an astrology magazine with the headline:

"You Can Predict Your Child's Future." Her cigarette scatters ashes all over the plate.

Daddy Dead's truck spits stones up the driveway. The door slams. Aunt Oink pulls her sweater tight and examines her boobs to make sure they're still there. When Daddy Dead stomps in, he passes us in the hall but doesn't see. I wear a black ski mask and black leotard from my Halloween costume. I've strapped my brother's holster around my hips. I keep my silver gun in one pocket, Knife's head pops out of the other. I see Daddy Dead whisper in Aunt Oink's ear.

"I don't know where she is. Probably out in that junk car," she says.

He brushes her boobs and she grunts. They don't see me but then my brother wakes up from a nap and throws G.I Joe from across the living room.

"Give me back my stuff!"

Aunt Oink points her finger at me.

"I told you to play outside!"

"Did not liar!" I say.

Daddy Dead walks toward me – his shadow growing larger with each step until it fills the wall and the ceiling. When I look up his eyes are blue with fire.

He doesn't really mean it. He shows off for Aunt Allie. My father isn't bad; he has troubles – Allie troubles and nightmares from the Jesus bottle.

"You don't talk back to your elders, you hear? Show some respect!" His eyes narrow and go hard. "Children should be seen and not heard."

"Maybe she needs a snack," Aunt Oink says and opens the refrigerator then unscrews the lid and walks toward me jiggling a pig's knuckle. The skin wrinkles from the vinegar and you can see the bone.

Daddy Dead never stops her. He's afraid of losing her boobs so he goes along.

I yank Knife from my holster and stick her in Aunt Oink's face.

"I wouldn't do that if I were you," I tell her.

We wear our clothes and shoes under the bed covers. I put some peanut butter, crackers and a banana in a lunch bag along with a map of Paris, France. I stole the map from the bookstore. When everyone is snoring, Knife and I sneak through the bedroom door and crawl to Aunt Oink's jewellery box. I twist the key slowly in the fancy gold keyhole. Aunt Oink snorts in her sleep. The photos are slick in my hand.

We slide along the hallway to the kitchen and slowly close the door. It's dark and all I can hear is the refrigerator rumbling. I slip my flashlight out and spotlight the stove.

"You're a military genius," I tell Knife.

We line the photos along the counter. First the one with Aunt Oink sprawled on the living room floor, bare naked except for a Vic Diamone album covering her pubic hair; then the one where she wears Daddy Dead's black leather jacket and nothing else, and last the photo where she holds her boobs up like pizza pies.

"Let's blow evil wolf breath on these."

We open our mouths and puff and the photos jump across the counter.

On the front of the oven is a small window. The glass is doubled so there is a space in between but we have to pry open the steel strip that holds it in place. We use a butter knife around a loose section just wide enough to slip the photos in one by one. There's just enough room for all three. Mother Blind can't miss them even with flour in her eyes. Aunt Oink and Daddy Dead will burn and curl into ash inside the oven.

Knife and I wait all night for daybreak. My baby sister sleeps wrapped in a pink blanket in her crib next to my bed. Mother Blind tucks her cover around her the way she wraps cabbage for "pigs in a blanket." I spit the meat part out and only eat the cabbage. All night we count cabbages in our heads waiting for daybreak. At about the three-thousand-and-thirty-third cabbage Mother Blind shuffles down the hallway and into the kitchen. I hear the faucet hiss, the coffee pot rattle and I hug Knife tight inside my jacket then coffee pot crashes to the floor and spins its lid then stops and it's dead quiet. It seems like a long time before Mommy screams.

We run for the window and jump.

The frying pan crashes and Mother Blind shouts:

"Filthy swine!"

I hear my father with his sleepy growl. "What the hell's going on here?"

"Jesus!" Aunt Oink hollers.

My baby sister screams.

We run to King Car and pry open the rusted door. I grab the steering wheel. We rock the car side-to-side, back and forth till it rumbles. Through the broken rear view mirror I see my mother, my aunt, my father in the ruined window.

"Don't look back!" Knife shouts.

I jam the gas pedal with the tips of my toes. The muffler smokes and the kitchen window floats away.

"Faster!" Knife says. Her left eye spins.

King Car lifts and comets and stars rush past the jelly jar window and light a path all the way to Paris.

The Red Dress
Anna May Mangan

Kitty explained to her neighbour in a flat voice, "It was a girl with a tiny head, shaped like a lemon with a balloon belly and too hairy to live. They're always hairy when they're so early." She was senseless with grief, warm blood still pulsing out between her legs and her breasts were crying milk… but no baby to heal her.

The nights were the worst each time. Her brittle sleep was disturbed by messages from her daughter. "She's trapped behind the wallpaper!" Kitty stood on the corner of the bed for hours, a demented figure clawing at the wallpaper and through to the plaster beneath, ripping her nails and tearing the skin on her fingertips. As she worked she called out to her baby girl to let her know that mammy was coming to get her and make her safe.

Finally the ambulance came for her, just as it had the times before, and Kitty was secured to a bed with a black rubber mattress cover that smelt of a blend of bleach and vomit. Her head was clamped as she convulsed repeatedly to the thunderbolts of ECT treatment at Mullingar Mental Hospital.
In part restored Kitty returned home a mere month later to find the wall above the bed had been replastered and repapered. Like the times before

it didn't match, but she couldn't care less. Her tiny, twisted last chance daughter had been erased from the memory of relieved family, friends and neighbours. But never hers.

Her Doctor damned Kitty by declaring her incapable of carrying a baby to full term. He included 'unstable' 'delicate' and 'nervy' into her diagnosis. Kitty crouched beneath his canopy of words and lived a quiet, low life. She looked well and less than her 42 years. She didn't turn heads, but then had never once tried to. She preferred to be left alone to concentrate on the turmoil inside her.

Even her husband, Jimmy, left her alone. He was a soldier and had been posted overseas to the Congo almost immediately after her last stay in the mental hospital. He had regular home visits but always volunteered to return to Africa.

She wasn't ever lonely for Jimmy, he wrote regularly. In one of his letters, which were invariably short, misspelt and only about himself he wrote the line "Just a line to let you know *who* I am". She believed he had intended to say *how* I am. A simple enough mistake for a poorly educated man but Kitty felt it very significant without being sure why. She kept that letter, and all the others went into the fire.

There were whispers that Jimmy and his friend had been visiting prostitutes when they went on local leave in the Congo. Kitty believed this because she had experienced Jimmy's desires at close quarters. She understood only too well that they were frequent, always urgent and exceedingly quick. She hoped he was paying the prostitutes by the minute, not the hour. They were supposed to be saving up for a trip to England.

Although she was legally bound to be the object of his desire Kitty categorised their brief coupling as being the equivalent for Jimmy of a good nose blowing or passing wind – 'better out than in'. Sex for him was an expulsive body function and she was the in-house recipient.
Many of the other wives grandly refused to give credence to the notion that their men were cavorting with prostitutes, largely because in a small town

in Ireland in 1958 a coupling between a white man and a black woman was unthinkable. Kitty succumbed to sinful fireside thoughts at times, including the puny Jimmy in his white cotton vest tucked into yellow streaked Y fronts ravaging an assortment of Amazonian, shiny black women with bones through their noses. To erase these troubling images Kitty later went to confession and admitted to her priest that she had entertained perverted thoughts about people who were poor and hungry. Father, in a puzzled tone, delivered her a penance of one Our Father and three Hail Marys.

When Jimmy's posting came to a permanent end he arrived home with a collection of brown medicine bottles full of bug shaped tablets. He carefully explained to her that all personnel returning from the Congo were at risk of contracting malaria. Kitty dutifully took charge of his doses, leaving the drugs next to his mug of tea each mealtime.

Kitty ran his weekly bath for him and saw the oozing sores on his penis. From the day he returned from the Congo, although they shared a bed each night he always lay with his back facing her, and he never reached for his wife. That was his way of taking care of her.

One early summer evening Jimmy had just eaten his usual fried egg and mash meal and wipes the plate clean with a fistful of her doughy homemade bread. He lifted his dish and carried it over the sink where Kitty stood wiping the pans clean. He had never done that before. Her senses all stood to attention at once, waiting for him to speak. "I have two tickets for the dinner and dance" he said.
"Why?"
"A night out will do you good. Get you out of the house."
She wanted to snap back that when she was cleaning the toilets and washing the waiting room floors at Moate station before dawn each day she was 'out of the house' thankyouverymuch. Instead she paused a moment and constructed a reply that would appeal to his innate miserliness and put an end to his proposal.
"I've got nothing to wear."
Jimmy beamed as if anticipating her words and nodded towards the couch. She followed the nod to see a package wrapped in brown paper. He had

been shopping! "Indeed and you have!" he declared.

The dress was red and gossamer light; different from anything she had ever worn. After her initial huffing embarrassment Kitty admitted to herself that she liked it and tried it on several times a day while he was at work.

The occasion was an informal army dinner dance for men returned from the Congo and their partners, more VD than VE thought Kitty. The atmosphere in the hall that was hung with paper chains and brightly coloured concertina lanterns was smoky and sparky. The roast beef dinner hot and tasty. Unaccustomed to being served Kitty was too polite to say 'no' to the young waitresses in their black and white uniforms and accepted several glasses of sweet white wine with her meal even though she rarely took alcohol.

As the evening went on and she watched the dancing from her table she was aware of her heavy sad spirit evaporating upwards into the ballroom. It rose and vanished into the swirl of laughter and talking and dancing. Towards the end of the night Kitty danced with Jimmy for the first time in over 15 years. Her dress was fluid and sheer, perfect for dancing. His rough hands spun her around and reeled her back to him in time with the music. He was confident and sure of the moves. Kitty was reluctant for the evening to end, and when it did she stepped into the street calling out goodnight to people she'd never spoken to before in a loud, cheery voice. Jimmy slipped his arm through hers and steered her home.

He was very quiet on the walk home and seemed to be looking at her more than usual. Every time she glanced sideways at him he was already watching her. The air and alcohol mix had made Kitty feel most peculiar, her gait changed and she began to walk as though there was soft sand beneath her feet. Aware that she was leaning on Jimmy, the red dress felt thin and alien against her body.

One of the songs played at the dance that evening had gone "There was a mouse, WHERE? There on the stairs, where on the stairs? Right there..." She had danced to it with abandon stamping her feet at the chorus. It entered her head again immediately as Jimmy pushed the front door open and she saw the stairs in double focus rising before her. She began to sing the song softly under her breath and stumbled and fell up the first few stairs. The song kept playing in her head as Jimmy swiftly, and without words, lifted her dress from behind and fumbled with his trousers before he climbed onto her back with a sudden frenzy of movement. Her head was turned to one side and her cheek got a carpet burn from the weight of his forehead pressing on her temple as he moved up and down, in and out. She smelt the familiar odour of alcohol that she associated with sex. In the past Jimmy had frequently got fired up after a few pints. This time, with her face pushed against the stair carpet that same smell was coming from her, too. She grunted in disgust, he grunted with pleasure.

Sleep fluttered all night and finally she came too, feeling exhausted. Her head pulsed painfully with every heartbeat and the daylight stung her eyes. Rolling over to get out of bed there was a sweaty soreness between her legs. Slowly she made the bed and picked up Jimmy's clothes from the floor and dropped them into the wash basket. Where was the red dress?

Jimmy had gone to work hours earlier and taken the red dress with him. He had tossed it into the bottom of the bucket for meat offcuts destined for burning.

Kitty knew almost immediately, the tips of her breast tingled and that had happened each of the four times before. The first so happy time she had described this sensation to a bemused Jimmy as her breasts singing! She blushed now at the memory and how rapt she had been.

Kitty delayed telling him until she was almost 6 months gone and only then because she was convinced he would discover it for himself by looking at her crescent shaped belly pushing out her clothes. She waited until after Sunday lunch when he was at his most relaxed, reclining in the armchair with a glass of stout and the newspaper laying open across his chest. He was halfway to a doze. In a high and trembling voice she said from the other side of the doorway "there's a baby on the way". Returning from his reverie he replied evenly, "Whose?"

She was rooted to the spot for the minutes it took him to respond. He stood from the chair stiff with rage and walked out of the house through the back door so he would not have to pass by her. He did not return home for a week.

She moved silently through the pregnancy. Every minute change in her skin and beneath it heralded to Kitty the beginning of the end. An itch could paralyse her with terror. At night she lay in bed with her eyes wide open, night after night anticipating a lightweight blue baby that would never meet her gaze, just like the others.

Even though Kitty was frozen by fear time moved on and tugged her with it. She spent most days sitting by the window her palms upturned on her lap. In that position she could see the pale pink scars, only shadows now, of the deep red welts from the straps that held her in place on the mattress for the ECT treatments.

She gazed without seeing out of the window, concentrating on the stirrings in her belly. She adored how it felt but could only imagine the baby as a torso; she was terrified to let it have a face or fingers in her imagination because they were what she had ached for when her dead babies had been taken away.

Kitty felt the familiar pop of her waters breaking, and her heart cracked at the same moment. She peeled back the hem of her dress and forced herself to look down. No blood? What does that mean? Stunned she got up from the chair, with great difficulty, and spoke to the room. "Make it different please God, make it different God…" she repeated this mantra style as she enjoyed the strong pains because they blunted her fear.

Kitty busied herself with routine tasks in the next couple of hours; she washed and curled her hair, made soda bread and tidied her pantry. She was relishing the pain and wanted to keep what was happening a secret between herself, God and the baby. Finally, doubled over in pain, when she knew her time was close and she didn't dare delay any longer, she went to the doorstep and called to a neighbour's child to run and fetch the doctor.

Doctor Block, who had delivered Kitty's four dead babies, gave the panting child a shilling to continue running to the priest's house so he could attend the birth immediately. Then he put together a small kit to assist with the labour and enable him to remove the baby's body from the house when delivery was complete.

He hurried into Kitty's house and on arrival was startled by the scene before him. Kitty was lying on her side on the sitting room floor with her dress pulled up to the middle of her back exposing her blood-streaked buttocks. The placenta was pulsing behind her, dark red and steaming.
She was shaking so violently he was certain she was in the throes of a convulsion. Hurling his bag to one side the Doctor rushed towards her praying silently under his breath.

Kitty wasn't having a convulsion, she was heaving with silent sobs that possessed her whole body. Clamped to her breast and sucking greedily was a plump and pink baby boy. Kitty was staring at the infant with wild unblinking eyes. She grasped him tight in both her arms and was unaware that the Doctor was in the room. The crown of the baby's head was covered in matted dark hair made shiny by the hot tears streaming from his mother's eyes.

Jimmy approached his house shortly after the Doctor. He gingerly pushed the door wide straining to hear what was happening inside. He turned into the front room from the hallway and saw the Doctor crouched over his wife's prone body and a wave of defeat swept over him. This time they were both dead.

He joined the weeping doctor at Kitty's side and his knees buckled when he saw his wife cradling his hearty baby son for the first time. Jimmy threw back his head and roared out, a sound that swamped the doctor's crying and the first lusty wails of the baby boy they called Declan Joseph Mellett.

Declan was christened in the first half hour of his life by the priest who had come to arrange his funeral.

Cold Cut
Alexa Beattie

The father said the boy had fallen. That the train had jerked forward all of a sudden and the boy, not paying attention, had lurched and blown out his cheekbone on the metal struts of the seat in front. That's what happened, the father said, popping the cap on a Pabst and putting it to his already moistened lips.

"Poor little guy," the uncle said, standing there. "Too bad," and took a beer for himself from the case in the refrigerator.

The children next door were skipping beneath a sprinkler, following under it as it arced slowly back and forth. In the afternoon sunlight, it was as if the drops were held together in one long glittering strand. Backwards and forwards. Backwards and forwards.

"Too bad about that face," said Bill, the uncle, gesturing toward the boy sitting with his back to them on the step. "A real shiner." The boy could hear clearly, but he kept his back turned. He listened to the sound of laughter coming from the children next door and watched the trail of an airplane as it inched its way across the spotless blue sky.

"Time for another," Bob said shaking his empty bottle from side to side like it was a bell he was ringing. As he went inside, the screen door rocked loudly in its frame.

"Another cold one, Bill?"

Bill didn't answer but Bob would bring him one anyway

In the kitchen where the women were, the light was fingering its way in through the slats in the blinds, shadows of leaves dappling thinly on the counter where the cigarettes and ashtrays were.

"Any cold ones going spare?" Bob said, already pulling on the refrigerator door. "You ladies, what are you drinking?"

"Barb and I were just talking," Sue said. "I was telling about our journey out here. The train and all. How that was."

Bob looked at his wife, but didn't say anything.

"You boys'll want some lunch, I bet," said Barb. "I've got some cold cuts in the fridge, some pickles and whatnot. We could make sandwiches. Would Frankie like a sandwich, do you think?"

Next door, the children were taking turns sliding down the grass to the sidewalk. The muddier their bodies became, the louder they shrieked. The father wiped the sweat off his bottle and pressed it to his brow. He plucked at the neck of his t-shirt where the u-shaped patch of moisture clung. The men had lit cigarettes and were holding them backwards, cupping them behind their hands like there was a strong wind they were trying to shield them from.

"It's a scorcher alright," Bill said, wiping his lip with a broad sweep of his tongue. "A real scorcher."

"So how'd he get that shiner, again?" Bill said, poking his beer in the boy's direction and holding on to the porch railing. "The train, you said. How was the train, anyway? That's a long-ass trip."

Bob said, Yes it was. But if you napped and took frequent trips to the dining car, it actually went by fast. Not too bad at all. "Should do it more often. Or else you guys come out and see us next time."

The boy was standing now, cupping his eye with his hand and holding his other arm out straight. He looked like he was checking his vision. How many fingers. In the brassy midday sunlight, the bruise looked almost pretty, all purples and blues and ever so slightly green. But the blood had seeped into his eye and was spreading inward towards the green of his iris, captured there like water under glass. It made him look like a boxer, only his frame was too small.

On the porch, the men were getting on to the subject of sports. Batting averages, standings, and so forth. They joshed a bit with each other and rolled back on their heels. They lit cigarettes and took down gulps of smoke.

"Fancy another?" Bob said, adding his bottle to the line of "dead soldiers" along the porch railing. He did that at home too and his wife didn't like it. She'd even brought out a cardboard box for empties because she said it didn't give a good impression to the neighbors. There were seven of them lined up, but the man couldn't remember who was winning.

Still with his good eye closed the boy was using his thumb to measure things: a tree, the Trans Am parked a few houses up and finally, the children dancing in and around the sprinkler. It was hotter now and the water from the sprinkler hitting the sidewalk sent up a thick muggy smell like rain on hot tarmac. Standing there, the boy looked for all the world like he might be aiming an arrow, or a gun. The children mostly didn't notice, or if they did only stopped to look for a moment or two. They weren't that much younger than him and in different circumstances might have invited him to play.

Bill knew lunch wasn't far off because he could hear the clatter of plates from the kitchen, the tinkle of knives and forks. Barb would be going out of her way to make things nice. It wasn't often they had company. He was feeling hot now. The sweat was running in beads down his back, and the idea of lunch in the cool dining room was appealing to him. He was watching the children in the water, their liberated play. He and Barb didn't know the neighbors that well even though they'd lived there some time. But Bill was sure to say, "Hi" when he saw them getting out of the car. They gave candy to the kids at Halloween. He liked to see them out like this, playing happily in the street. It reminded him of when he was a kid.

Someone had taken the sprinkler off the hose and now all hell had broken loose. The little boy had it and, by putting his thumb over the hole, made chaotic squirts that were sending the girls running. Frankie had stopped his measuring and had gone to sit down on the grass between the two houses. It was almost as if, in this heat, he wanted to get hit, to be as drenched as they were.

"Five minutes 'till lunch, boys," Barb shouted from inside. "Better be hungry."

"Hear that, Frankie" Bill said. "Lunch in a few."

Frankie still had his back to the men. He was watching the little boy hold the hose more like a pistol and blasting it into the bodies of his sisters. He could feel the blood in his eye as a tightness, like his eye was bulging. Where the skin had broken beneath the eye, the blood was dark and clotted like whatever had hit him had done a damn good job.

Bob said he was starving. That there was nothing like travel to give him an appetite. He said he hoped Barb would have made her famous potato salad.

"That sister of mine sure can cook," he said, snapping the bottle out of his mouth and holding it up in a mock toast.

When Sue came out to say lunch was ready, she looked at Bob and the bottles, and then at Frankie who was still sitting on the lawn between the two houses. The children had stopped their water games and were sitting on the steps stripping bits of candy rope. One of them looked at Frankie and gave a quarter smile. Then he got back to his stripping. The girls looked around then and one of them waved.

Sue and Barb had been having their own little party in the kitchen, smoking cigarettes and loosening up with their talk. They weren't really drinking, just smoking, taking puffs between chopping or whatever it was they were doing. Barb said it was a shame about poor Frankie and wondered how long eyes like that lasted. Did they manage to ice it on the train, she asked. It must have hurt, she said, falling on metal like that. Was there anything she could give him to make him feel better? Just one of her lunches would do the world of good, Sue said, hooking her finger into the potato salad.

"Mmmm, just like I remember."

Out on the porch, Bill looked at the sky and said he thought there might be a storm coming. The clouds had banked up and some of them were looking dark around the edges. But they could use the rain, Bill said, gesturing towards a band of yellowing perennials. "It's been a helluva summer what with all this drought."

Bob said it was the same back East and tocked his butt into one of Bill's planters where, through the leaves, it sent up a fine thread of smoke. He was just about to head in for another beer when Sue came out to the porch to say that lunch was ready.

"Where's Frankie?" she said, seeing him sitting on the grass. The children had gone inside and the street was quiet. Frankie was ripping tufts of grass and tamping them back into the soil. Ripping and tamping, ripping and tamping.

"Where's Frank," Sue said again as if she couldn't actually see what she was staring at. "It's lunchtime."

As they sat down, the first drops were starting to fall, smacking the air conditioning unit in the window and making a tinny sound. Barb had already brought out the potato salad and was now bringing the platter of sandwiches.

"Sue made these," she said, parking the platter in the middle of the table. "Turkey or beef."

"Speaking of beef," Bill said. Hadn't he heard that it was good for black eyes. That a nice slab of rare meat held against the eye like a compress worked wonders. When he suggested they try it now, Barb said he was drunk and it was a disgusting idea.

"You could kind of see how it would," Bill said. "I mean blood on blood, nice and cold. Could work well for sporting injuries, too."

Bob didn't appear to be listening. He was tinkering with his sandwich, using his fork to hook the pickle out. The tomato. It looked like he was thinking about his sandwich, lost in thought and not listening to Bill's talk about beef and black eyes. Next, he pulled out the beef and piled it to the side of his plate, like he wasn't going to eat it. Like he was saving it for something.

Looking at Bob, Sue said she was sure the eye would be better in the morning, that black eyes always looked worse than they are.

"Yes," said Barb, "it was really mostly surface."

"Sure looks that way, anyhow," Sue said.

Frankie had helped himself to potato salad and was eating his sandwich. He was listening to the drum beat the rain on the air conditioning sent up–boom-boom, boom-boom, boom-boom, boom-boom–and tapping his finger in time.

Bob reached for another sandwich and Bill said, "Dig in." He also said all that travel must have built up an appetite in them. "I know it does me."

Barb said everyone should make room for dessert, especially Frankie, because she'd made something special. She looked outside, the raindrops on the windows, the dripping leaves, the sodden, bruised sky.

"Will this rain ever let up," she said, even though, really, it had only just begun.

My Friend Joe
David Mohan

In one continuous curve in August in the summer of 1996 in my beat up car, I drove myself off the road between San Diego and Dallas, and into the sizzling hot grass of a Texas wheat field.

Months later I'm sitting in the kitchen in my mama's trailer in my hometown, Mayfield, watching her prepare breakfast.

'That beautiful car,' she moans. 'Just what got into that head of yours?'

'None of your business,' I say, as though I'd had a special reason. I get real busy turning my coffee cup round and round on the table top, letting the stains it leaves on the old Formica overlap and loop like one of those child's spirogimminies.

She sighs a bit more at that, and stirs her pan. 'I can't figure it. A grown man and you've got to take the bus just to get to work.'

'My Jesus Christ, Mama. That car was a Grade A piece of shit.'

'It was not,' she says, almost immediately, pouncing like a puma. 'It was the one good thing that you ever had. You took that car to all around, up to Mexico. New Orleans. How'd you do all that otherwise? Tell me that.'

'The train,' I say, 'just like everybody else without a car.'

'But you had a car, Brandon, you had a car,' she says, as though I was some kind of retard.

My spirogimminies pattern is somewhat convoluted up at this stage. As always, when talking with my mother, I am beginning to lose my reason.

'Is that ready yet?' I ask, just to change the subject, 'You've been stirring that pan so much you're making me dizzy.'

'Soon enough,' she mutters, continuing to stir. 'You should be fixing up to go to work soon anyway.'

Her words, as always, make me wince. That's my latest job in town she's talking about. I've gone through the rest mostly at some point or other. This one—lugging crate boxes round some factory floor—is just nearly killing me, and is coming just as unstuck as all the others. I crumple up my face a bit more, just to let her know the gravity of my situation.

'I'm pretty much fixed on quitting the job up at Langford's, since you're asking,' I put out casual, ready to hear her moan some more.

'Well you do that Brandon,' she says resignedly, 'and that's where you'll be.'

She picks up the big old spoon she'd been using to provoke our breakfast and places it down softly on her kitchen counter, all as though she'd really meant to place it there ever so gently, though I know she'd been planning on slamming it there, and takes off into her bedroom like the quarrelsome witch she is.

Despite a lifetime of it, or perhaps because of that, I take a disinclination to the grits congealing in mama's pan. On account of having some taste buds left perhaps. Instead, I swing my jacket on and am making a half-assed getaway when the flimsy door rips open a crack.

Mama's head sticks out, as sore looking as a bent thumb, 'And don't you even think of bringing that girl here again tonight.' My mama keeps a fierce lid on that temper of hers, but she still makes the word 'girl' sound like something horrendous.

'Uh-huh,' I say in my joshing way, and trip out the door as slick as a rodeo.

A cool, serene spring morning in the trailer park. I skirt past the Sager's spilt-over water-tank, hup through two yards, then it's a quick hop over the wall to the bus depot.

The bus into Mayfield is irregular at best, except in the morning, with half the park heading into town. I jog a little in the chill of the late morning, then put my jacket on. I am patting the pockets to find my smokes when a small crackle alerts me to Joe Buckram's letter, the thing I'd clean forgot. Old Joe, from way back; we'd hung out in high school. Joey Buckram and me, we'd been buddies in the day, hitching around up to no good, you know how it is. He'd hauled off since, years past, moved himself out to Austin. We'd lost touch. A long, long time ago, it was. The letter went:

Hey Brandon G.,

What's cooking? Coming up March 6th for pa's funeral. Meet you in Pete's for the old schmo. I'll be in your usual seat—head to the bar most like. Mom's beat up about it, so don't try charming no one if you go up to the farm.

Joe

I'd been reckoning on skipping work today anyway, but this decides it. I scrunches it up again, feeling sort of regretful and sad about things as they'd been and now as they were. I'd never gone up to see his mama neither, so he'd needn't worried himself about me charming anyone, man or beast.

The bus came eventually, the driver chewing gum with a venomous look. I sit back and hitched my knees up on the edge of my seat just to get comfortable. The view from the bus into town is pretty much country—the town itself ain't that much more when truth get told. In a short while, not short enough, this countryside falls away to reveal downtown Mayfield in all its dubious glory. Believe me when I say this is pretty much always a disappointment even for the fresh-faced first timer. There's not much when you step off to let you know you've arrived. A liquor store for the town drunks – a considerable proportion of the population – a titty bar, a hoedown hall. All the staples of country life in other words.

I walk a bit up the not much-of-a main street. They've got all the kinds of shops you don't want or don't need: a florist, a haberdashers, a country ladies' boutique. I pass an old couple strolling by arm in arm like sweethearts—quaint and charming if you're passing by, depressing if you happen to live here.

I've got some time to kill I reckon—Joe was never much of an early drinker, so I take a nice, health-enhancing stroll myself, off the track a little to skirt the edges of the creek. This is the sort of wholesome thing I rarely do, but it's that sort of day so I think I might risk it.

I head back then, for real this time, thinking as I light up on the way, that that's more than enough fresh air for one morning. This time I head straight for old Pete's—if I've got to wait some, I'll wait in a sociable way. Pete's has got that slightly derelict, queasy look a bar has in the morning. It's dark inside, and there's no one there besides Pete himself and old Bill Farley, who's pretty much a fixture. I stride up to the bar. Old Bill is clearing his throat in that indulgent way he has. When he does that you know you're in for some sort of god-awful yarn from way back about moonshine distilling in the years of the depression.

Pete smirks at me a bit, no doubt wondering how even I could be propping up a bar with the birds just fresh awoken in the trees.

'What's it to be Mr Gannaway?'

'A Coke most like,' says Bill, as husky as a freight train.

'Make it the same as usual,' I say sharply.

'What's got you out of your box anyways Gannaway? Your mom will be fit to stitch a skunk. Isn't that right, Bill?'

'Sure is.'

'So what you been up to Gannaway? Still working up at Langford's in your spare time.'

'Kind of,' I say somewhat distracted, 'I've been thinking to take myself on the road again perhaps, work on the ranches.'

'Ranching,' says Pete, a bit sceptical, but humouring me just the same. Then breaking into a wicked smile, he says, 'Our friend here thinks he's some kind of cowboy.'

Bill cackles at that, somewhat predictably.

'I do not,' I say, feeling a real resentment brewing. 'Though it's a wonder you're still any sort of barman. This beer tastes like shit.'

Pete guffaws at that. 'That's off the back of last night most like,' he says, assuming his barman slouch, leaning back against the sink, his fat butt heaving over the edge of it. 'You should have had some breakfast first.'

'I wasn't hungry. Now, Jesus H can you talk about something else?

I head over to the jukebox with my beer, letting the boys get on with it. It's something of a ploy—I know this jukebox inside out, have heard every song on it a thousand times, but I'm looking to slide over to some dark corner I can bring Joe to, to talk in private. No use the whole town knowing the other half of my business it don't already know. I make a play of looking over some old Motown classics then settle myself quietly down on one of Pete's fancier fake-velvet seats.

I look up and there he is almost standing over me, too large as life to quite take in. He must have slipped in when I was fussing about with Marvin Gaye and Aretha Franklin. I look up at him for a moment recognising and not recognising him all at once and thinking why the fuck he came so formal in a suit and all, and then I remember he's come straight, most probably, from his daddy's funeral. Even with the suit, I start to think, he's not half as flash as I'd been expecting.

'Hey there, country bumpkin,' he says.

'Hey, look at you city slicker,' I fire back at him, not quite knowing what's expected for this scene straight out of *Days of Our Lives*. Should I hug him just like a long lost brother? I settle for a rough, joshing handshake instead and even at that he looks at me strangely.

'So there,' I say, suddenly nervous for no reason, knowing Pete and Bill will be watching us now and recording for the sake of gossip every lick of the scene.

'Well now,' says Joe. He smiles with white city teeth. 'What you keep looking at,' he says, looking at the bar.

'Oh, hit don't matter,' I say, taking off Bill a bit, 'I'm just looking at those two fools over there speculating over the fine-looking women they glimpsed a thousand years ago in Clay City.'

He laughs at that a bit, and exclaims, 'Yessir, oh my gosh,' as another tribute to old Geronimo.

'You hold tight there,' he says, 'I'll round them in this time,' and he goes to fetch up some more liquor to our table, and I get my first moment to think awhile since he pounced on me, all unawares.

Now here was Joe. This was Joe. Joe Buckram. But this was a different Joe. He looks as mighty fine as the women liked back in the day, but he's just a bit crumpled too—though positively less so than me. A city boy now, definite. I can tell already or I strongly suspect. He's lost the country about him, that's why he's so busy putting it on.

'Here we are, here we are,' he says, scuttling in with a raft of beers. 'What you up to anyhow,' he asks, arranging the glasses in a little ring upon the table, just like a wagon train making camp.

'On this fine summer morning?'

'Exactly.'

'Nothing much'. I sees no way round it. 'Dodging work for a spell.'

'Oh righty. Where you working?'

'Langfords, and I'll tell you for nothing I'd rather be unemployed and lying on the cold stones than taking another kicking from that family.'

'Same as usual then. Just the same old Mayfield,' observes Joe.

'Sure is. Won't change till Judgement day most likely unless they tear it down and do us all a favour.'

'So,' I says, 'down to says bye to the pops.'

'Yup.'

'Not much else would bring you back I'd imagine, Mr. Slick. What you driving now, anyways.'

'A big ole jeep.'

'Steady there. Fancy, fancy. How's things trucking up in Austin?'

He laughs a bit more at that, for no good reason, just like in the old days. I was always the joshing one at school, and Joe, Joe out of all of us was always the clever one. Mr. Brains we called him—and in the end it was no joke, he got out and quicker than a jackrabbit. You can't get cleverer than that.

'Not bad, not bad. I'm doing OK—got myself a nice little house in town, a smart little job in the city.'

'Sounds dandy.'

'It's OK.'

'You miss your daddy,' I ask out of an effort at politeness.

He wrinkles his face up at that, as though taken by painful recollection or just considering. 'Truth be told, Bran, not much. We were never that close. You know that.'

'Yeah, but he was your daddy just the same.' I say that for the sakes of those of us who never knew their daddy in the first place.

'True enough. But I've got as much family as I need back home.'

I digest that a bit, reddening for some reason along the way and thinking how curious it is to hear him call that far off city home.

'You've got a family then, have you? Kids hopping round?'

He laughs again, and it's starting to bug me.

'No kids, no. And you?'

'None and counting.' And that, my friend, is how it's gonna stay.'

'I hear you. I see they kept the creek nice at least, unlike most of the rest of town,' he says, pushing his chair in comfortably.

'Just the same as usual I suppose. Mostly the same as before as you can see,' I say stretching my legs out a bit. 'Nothing much has changed—for the better, at least.'

I look up and see his face is much stiller than my talk is, as though he were actually listening to deep silence. I come to a halt.

His eyes go down to the floor, like he's mimicking some demure widow at a county fair. I get to feeling a bit awkward, not knowing how to go on.

'Is it your daddy you're worrying at?' I say, reverting to unfamiliar territory—sympathy.

'No. Not that at all. Bran, you remember those summers when we were kids.' He starts talking in a low voice, earnestly. All about those long-gone, high school days of us and our gang hanging out and scooting round the dirt track roads in his daddy's old car and I begin to lose the thread of it through half-listening, feeling now, suddenly uncomfortably sure of what he's getting to. I know it when he comes to it at last as I knew he would.

'Remember that night that summer when we went swimming at the reservoir.'

'Man,' I say, suddenly more than perplexed, standing up, warmth rising from my feet up to the growing heat in my face, half lifting me from my chair. 'Man.' Pete and Bill's eyes flick over as fast as summer lightning, so I sit down again sharpish.

'Joe boy, I've told you a million times if I told you once I don't want to hear about that again. It's no use. You know that and I know that. So just let it rest.' I sit back with my beer clutched to my chest.

'I'm just remembering, Bran,' Joe puts in, looking a bit self-righteous. 'That's all.'

'Well don't.'

'I won't then. Jesus Christ.' he exclaims in an exasperated voice as though observing to himself, 'These fucking ditchwater towns. I just don't know.' I sit that one out, not knowing either. He looks over at me all agitated, squinting in the shadow. 'What's got into you anyway?'

'Nothing. Nothing's got into me. That's all. Not one thing.'

He looks hard at me then, then makes a show of looking at his watch. 'I reckon I'll go then. Should be heading back this afternoon anyway.' He stands up all in a hurry all of a sudden. It startles me a bit, but I don't let on. Let him make a disgraceful exit if he likes—I'll stay as cool as my cheap beer.

'Well, I'm heading then. See you round.' He puts his head down a bit to see me in the half-dark as though he was a chaplain or I was simple or a child.

'Keep on trucking.' I wave sullenly and shut my eyes tight a moment to give him sufficient time to saunter off. I hear a word or so passed between those two losers up at the bar and the phlegmy racket of Bill coughing up a storm.

When my eyes open up the place is empty again. He's gone and sauntered out, and for some reason I decide I'd better try to say my goodbyes proper so I speed out the bar as fast as a bear after a possum and just miss the dusty screech of his jeep setting off onto the dirt road, just a bit down the street. I run up a bit and get alongside just as he's setting off.

I call out something, patting the sides of a window while I can, until it suddenly speeds off too fast for me and I'm left half-running breathless behind. Most likely he didn't hear me because he's playing some travelling music on the radio or he's watching the road or something. I'm up the street a bit and so I sit down in the dirt of the roadside in the scorched grass and taking big deep breathes to help me calm myself, I listen to the long hot summer silence.

Eddie
Nikita Nelin

Eddie Gerialdo carefully cleans off the slimy rubber that lines the detergent cavity of a heavy duty laundry machine. Eddie is concentrating, and because these machines are large, his hands are shoulder level and the muscles in his neck are tense from the motion; and because he has bad eyes, he leans into the effort.

Eddie moves from one machine to another, and after the slime and residue powder are gone he will wipe the lint trays – Eddie has sixty-eight washing machines and eighty dryers – and then he will take out the garbage; and because he talks to himself, customers will stare, but because he has been here for close to a year, fewer and fewer will do so, and because when he walks his head lugs forward, and his arms ambiguously hang at his sides, and his hands bunch naturally into fists, no one will make eye contact.

Out with the garbage Eddie takes a break, but Eddie only walks to the end of the block and stands at the intersection before turning back, Eddie walks with his left foot dragging behind because there was once a hole in his thigh and a stringy patch of muscle has remained deformed. And because there are stipulations, Eddie has to tell Cabriela when he goes off duty. And because the avenue is almost empty, because it is dark, because it is late fall, because his hands are pocketed in his jacket, Eddie feels quiet, Eddie does not want to rush, Eddie counts his steps.

Because people come in and out of the Laundromat all night, Eddie stands still, letting them pass. And because he knows the layout and thinks of white dominos and monochrome tiles, his body wants to move forward; and because many of the customers are new they don't have a rhythm to the place, and Eddie feels his chest wanting to continue his route through the Laundromat, but because he scares people, he plants his feet, spreading them shoulder width, and his forehead masks his eyes, and he keeps a look of bemusement on his face, and his hair is cropped very short; because he stood in lines for ten years, because the cell locked at ten, because he shared a 12 x 6 stone room; because he was small, because for a long time he attracted attention, because his father once stood at a doorway with a loose eye and Eddie's blood on his forearms; because, Asiando paid well and Eddie was efficient; because he did not hesitate, because he was quiet, because his eyes hang low, and because he knows where the weak points are; Eddie avoids eye contact with the customers but the customers always feel like he is watching them. And Eddie is low to the ground; he knows where everyone is stepping.

At midnight Eddie's cousin Sunny comes by and leans on a stone column, and Sunny leaves his SUV idling outside. Sunny stares at Eddie, and Eddie takes out another pair of cleaning gloves. Though Eddie did not ask, Sunny talks about the neighborhood, and his new girl, and she is seventeen, and he calls her his Mulatta, and she lets him do anything, and Sunny needs help, and help is someone you can trust, and they used to trust Eddie; and because Sunny just talks about family, and the young girl, and the old park, and handball, and never mentions why he is here, Eddie knows what Sunny wants.

Because the machines run louder when Sunny is here, because Eddie knows that Sunny is staring at him while he mops the floor; because Eddie took the charge, and Eddie was always a low talker, and Eddie gets lost in the shadows, and Sunny does not want to know what happened; and at 2 am Cabriela's nephew Antonio will come by, and he has a silver cross hanging from his neck, and he smiles like the world does not matter but does not matter in a way entirely different from Sunny's; because Cabriela is always happy to see Antonio, and Antonio brings her spiced pork rice in a container, and Siela, Antonio's wife, made flan, and she asked Antonio to bring some for Eddie, and it is in a plastic container, and Antonio makes eye contact, and his chest is free, and he tells Eddie that the Mets lost, and Eddie has seen him play soccer on Saturdays, and all the machines seem to be set on wash cycle when he is here, and Cabriela turns on the soap-opera channel at 3 am, and Eddie sits next to her with the flan, and she laughs through him, and she gasps, and she yells at the screen when she finds out that Doctor Rodriga has been cheating on Solidar with nurse Tiffany and Tiffany is pregnant, and Doctor Rodrigo is not the sort of man who loses control, and he will arrange it so he is the one to deliver the baby, and the mother will die in birth, and the baby will be sent to a nunnery, and the nunnery has a garden and the sun falls soft yellow during volunteer hours, and Solidar, because she feels alone, because her husband is working overtime on his promotion, volunteers at the garden, and Solidar's womb is still; and Eddie does not say anything while Cabriela watches, and she is okay with that, and he eats, and she is animated, she is large, she has black creases at the corners of her eyes, she has a mullet; and because it could have been a throwaway container, but it isn't, and Eddie will wash it and bring it back next shift, because Eddie feels calm in the wash cycle, because it was all back then, because Eddie never remembers his dreams, and because the flan has figs in it, Eddie never asks Sunny to say why he is here.

Because people are afraid of Eddie, and he talks to himself, and he avoids eye contact. Eddie talks low, his speech is impaired, and words do not roll but hiss out in a humble monotone; and Eddie does not dream, he likes it cold, likes the rumbling of the wash cycle. Eddie walks weird, Eddie has a hole, and Eddie hangs his forehead. Because Eddie is always prepared, because, because quiet Eddie, because Eddie stays here, and Eddie does not cross the intersection; and because Sunny waits for Eddie, because the mulatto girl screams, and Eddie eats the flan, and the winter is coming, and Eddie works through the night, Eddie has brown eyes, and Eddie is on break. And because Eddie hears voices, because he can't puzzle them out, because they say Eddie, over and over, over, and over. Again.

Bernie McGill
No Angel

The first time I saw my father after he died I was in the shower, hair plastered with conditioner, when the water stuttered and turned cold. He was at the sink in front of the misted-up mirror with the tap running, his back to me. It was two weeks after his funeral. His things were all where he'd left them.

'Them tiles would need re-grouting,' he said, and pointed his razor at the salmon pink mould that was growing below the mirror.

I stared at him through the circle I'd wiped in the shower door. 'I didn't know you'd be able to do that,' I said.

'Oh yes,' he said, 'any decent tradesman would sort that out for you.' The twitch of a smile; thran as before.

He looked more or less the same. When he turned his face to scrape the razor along his jaw, I could see that the scar was healing well where the surgeon had removed the growth from the side of his nose. His skin was still yellow maybe more so at the nicotine-stained finger tips.

'Are they treating you well?' I asked him.

'So, so. The food's not great. Nothing seems to have much of a taste.'

'I suppose you empty the salt cellar over it still?'

'What harm's it going to do me now?'

I looked at him, at the thin white hair curling at the back of his neck from the steam in the bathroom; the earth under his fingernails.

'I'm getting cold,' I said.

'Don't worry,' he said, bending to splash water on his face, his knees creaking, 'I'm going now anyway,' and away he went.

The next time I saw him, I was on the train, on the way to Belfast sitting opposite a girl in a green bobble hat, when his face appeared in the window to my left. I looked back at the girl in her small round glasses, breaking off squares of chocolate with her teeth, at the umbilical iPod threading its way from her ear to her pocket. But outside, reflected in the glass, it was his face skimming over the fields. It was early December; there was a skin of snow on the hedges, green showing through; a slick of ice on the flooded grass. A bad time to spread slurry, he would have said. I'd never been on a train with him before.

'We used to ride to Knockarlet,' he said smiling his crooked smile, showing a bottom row of neglected teeth. 'Me and your mother. Left the bikes at the station and took the train to the Port for the Big Sunday. It's years since I was on a train.' He spoke the way he had always spoken in his later years, like he was suppressing wind, like the next sound that emitted from his mouth might be an involuntary one. People used to finish his sentences: he made them nervous of what was going to come out.

I loved that photo we had in the house, the pair of them strolling down the prom arm in arm, her in her swing coat and curled hair, him in his wide lapels, a cigarette hanging off his right hand. They looked like film stars; the ghosts of their young selves. I used to pore over it as a teenager, wondering who they had been then, before me and then Robbie were born into their lives; before we wrenched love from them, and left again.

Above his head in the train window, were mirrored the orange letters of the information screen: 'Attention please. Passengers without a valid ticket please purchase one from the conductor.' He looked up, stuck out his elbow, nudged no-one in particular, winked in at me: 'Never let on you saw me!' he said.

Christmas week, I was invited out to dinner with Thomas's parents. Situation vacant: prospective daughter-in-law. I watched them process my details: a good lecturing job, attentive, soft-spoken, a bit long in the tooth for grandchildren, possibly, but these days you never know. They were far too middle-class for religion to be an issue. The restaurant was over-heated; I'd gulped down too many glasses of *pinot grigio* and had stepped outside for a breath of air. Daddy legged it out from a bus shelter on the far side of the road; dodged over between breaks in the headlights, a greasy brown paper bag in his hand.

'Are you going to marry thawn boy?' he said. Not so much as a 'Hullo'.

'You know his name, Daddy.'

'Are you going to marry him?'

'He hasn't asked me.'

He sighed through his nose, and his breath came out in two puffs of mist. 'I never knew you were that oul-fashioned,' he said. The smell of chip fat and vinegar.

'What's in the bag?' I asked him.

'You didn't answer me.'

'Neither did you.'

A couple came out the restaurant door; a blast of voices and garlic and alcohol.

'He'll never set foot on my farm,' he said.

'He's a Maths teacher, Daddy. He doesn't want your farm.'

'He says that now,' he grunted. 'But they're all the same – hungry land grabbers every last one of them. He'll not get it. Not after what we went through to keep it.' He wrung the paper bag into a twist, fired it into a nearby bin.

'Not everybody's after your land, Daddy.'

'Have you forgotten what they did to your brother, Annie? The way they left him, lying on the road like a bag of rubbish the binmen had forgotten to lift? What it did to your mother, to see him like that?'

I gritted my teeth. 'It wasn't Thomas did that.'

'Him or his kind. I make no difference between them.' The spit flew out of his mouth. Then he turned on his heel and strode down the street, some loose change heavy in the outside pocket of his green fleece, banging against his thigh, altering the hang of him. It had never occurred to me that the dead could be bitter still, could still feel loss.

My brother Robbie wasn't the son my father had had in mind for himself. Daddy was a teetotaller all his life; the only drink we ever had in the house was a drop of poteen he kept for a sick cow. And my father was quiet, rarely raised his voice, except maybe to curse at a referee, or a traffic warden. Robbie, on the other hand, was loud, drank too much, lost all his money on poker machines, stole fags out of Daddy's coat pocket, took no interest in cattle rearing. He had a great sense of himself as unquashable, shot his mouth off when the rest of us knew how to stay dumb; he had never learnt caution the way most people had in our uneasy mixed community. Some of the time I admired him for it; wished I could speak without looking to the left and right of me first. He wasn't involved in anything, people round here would have known that: if he had been, Daddy would have knocked it out of him himself. All he wanted was to join a rock band and 'get the hell out of this backwater'. The eighties were a nervous time, and things were worse after something big: Loughgall, Enniskillen, Milltown, Ballygawley. Those were the times when people walked about careful, eyes to the ground. Robbie never eyed the ground. You'd think, then, he'd have seen it coming, what hit him in the face. A mallet, the coroner said, the type that was used to bash in fenceposts. They never found it.

Strange thing, though, he walked like Daddy: shoulders forward, great loping strides. Three years younger than me, and every step of his was one and a half of mine. I could never keep up with him. He was seventeen and built like a stick and mad about his guitar. He'd just failed his driving test and had called in the pub, where he shouldn't have been, and was walking home. They must have followed him out. It was December, dark by four and bone-cold. The coroner said he thought a car had hit him: after the beating, he said, when he had been left on the road. He couldn't be sure but there was evidence the body had been dragged. It was a neighbour that found him, picked him out in the car headlights. Daddy insisted on an open coffin, despite Robbie's eyebrow like a burst plum, his buckled nose, the rainbow of bruises that spanned his battered face. Despite Mum saying, 'Let people remember him the way he was.'

'No,' he'd said. 'Let everybody see what they did to him. Let everybody look and know what animals we're living amongst.'

They never got anybody for it, but ever since, there have been neighbours of ours that couldn't look us in the eye. Mum lasted six months of barely speaking, food hardly passing her lips. She dropped like a stone one day in the kitchen; never spoke again. 'Your mother,' Daddy said to me, like he had to apologise for her leaving, '… her heart never mended.' Then it was just me and him, for nearly twenty-two years, until his lungs gave way, and the breath left him too.

In one of the bad times, around Hallowe'en, a month or two before Robbie was killed, I was home from university and Mum asked me to go in the front room and bring her in the sewing basket that she kept under the bed. I knelt down on the burgundy carpet, lifted the valance sheet, and there was the shotgun, quiet as you like. Daddy had always kept one: he and Uncle Joe went shooting for pheasant every Boxing Day. And if there was a wedding in the townland, he'd take it out; shoot a cartridge or two in the air to send the bride off. But the rest of the time, he kept it locked up in the built-in wardrobe. He was normally very careful about it. I carried the basket back in to the kitchen.

'Why's the gun under your bed?'

'Thread that for me, will you?' she said. She sat with Daddy's good trousers on her lap, pressing the unravelled hem between her finger and thumb. I held the needle up to the light, laced the grey thread through.

'Two or three times,' she said, 'a car has driven into the yard at night. No lights; we hear the wheels on the gravel.' She took the needle from me, wound a knot into the end of the thread. 'Your father says if any of them tries to get in, he'll shoot first, ask questions later.'

'Why would anybody…?'

'There's people, Annie, that needs no excuse. We're the wrong sort for them, that's all; in the wrong place. They'd like to see the back of us.' And she pushed the needle into the hem and started to sew.

I was glad to get back to Belfast. The threat in the city never felt personal. A bomb scare on University Road and everybody piled back into bed, lectures cancelled for the morning. The night the explosion went off at the Lisburn Road police station, the whole of our rented house shook. Eight girls on the landing in their pyjamas and then down to the kitchen to stand bare-footed on the cracked, snail-slimed lino, warming our hands around cups of tea, listening for the sirens; second-hand drama. Not like a dark car in your own yard at night; not like a shotgun under the bed.

The next time I saw my father after he died it was night and I was driving over the bog road near Castlenagree with the windscreen wipers doing battle against the rain and Bob Dylan on the radio, 'Like a Rolling Stone'. I'd turned the music up full and was giving it welly: 'How does it feel…?'

'What's that oul' shite you're listening to?' he said, and near put me off the road. A twitter of a laugh: 'That would cleave you,' and his arm reached out, and turned down the dial. The dashboard gave off a green light; my fists tight on the steering wheel. 'What happened your hand?' he said. A small black crescent of soot was ingrained above my knuckles.

'You know rightly what happened it,' I told him, 'putting the life out of me in the coal house last night. I hit it against the shovel.' He was silent. The sound of his skin-roughened finger and thumb, rubbing together. 'Knocking the door against the back of my heels,' I said. 'You know I don't like the dark.'

'It was maybe the wind.'

'There wasn't a breath. You needn't deny it. I smelt Benson and Hedges.'

'I've given up the smokes,' he said. 'They were a shocking price, getting.'

'Your timing's not great.'

The rain was coming down harder, troughing water along the sides of the road. I could smell the damp wool of his jacket, drying in the fan, and something underneath it, something familiar - coal tar soap.

'Does this seat not go back?' he said, grappling for the lever at the side, 'That Thomas boy must be a right short-arse. My knees is killing me.' I was silent, not rising to the bait, and then, 'Do you remember,' he said, 'the night you swallowed the two-p bit?'

I did. I was five, six maybe. I can still feel the chink of metal against my teeth, taste the copper, feel the wrong shape of it slide down my throat. I don't know what upset me more: the swallowing of it, or the disappointment at the loss of the money. I hadn't made the connection between food and waste; was stunned when Mum said I wasn't to flush the toilet till she was sure it had passed. And every morning, the same line from him and Robbie…

'Any change?' he said in the seat beside me, his whole body shaking.

That was the night he told me the story of Ali Baba and the Forty

Thieves. And when he reached the part about the robbers hiding in the urns, I didn't know the word, so he said, 'You know, urns, big containers, like tea chests. That's what we'll call them. The thirty nine robbers hid in the tea chests and the captain went into the house.' It was nearly worth swallowing the coin for: the candy-striped sheets in their big bed, and the light coming in under the crack in the door and 'Ali Baba' in his turban and the blind cobbler and the clever servant-girl and the robbers in the tea chests. And the burst-open brother they had to sew back together again.

'You know, Annie. I would never scare you like that. That wasn't me at the coal house door.'

I kept my eyes on the road as we rounded a bend. Then I said, 'Daddy, do you ever see…?' but when I turned my head, the seat beside me was empty.

He needn't have bothered with the jibes about Thomas: we didn't last. I think it was Thomas's confidence I fell for - his belief in my ability to love him back, his faith in the world's acceptance of us both. He never questioned his right to be anywhere. He was entirely without arrogance but he stood and talked and put one foot after the other with absolute unshakeable conviction. I think, maybe, if I'm honest, he reminded me of Robbie. It was never going to work. I couldn't have kept up the suitable daughter-in-law show for a whole lifetime.

Daddy made occasional appearances after that. One Tuesday afternoon after the spring term had started, I looked out from a lecture hall of second-year students who cared little for Molière or the Commedia dell'Arte and I saw him, intent, climbing a grass bank, heading towards the University Arboretum with a hazel stick in his hand, his corduroy trousers bagging at the knees. I got the impression he was following someone.

Then one night in May at the Opera House, a staff outing to *The Bartered Bride* and me bored witless, I tore my eyes away from Marenka in her embroidered apron and glanced up at the boxes and there he was: good grey suit, opera glasses in his hand. He who had never set foot in a theatre in his life.

'What are you doing here?' I mouthed up at him.

'Keeping an eye on him,' he said and he stuck out his elbow and nudged the man beside him: Robbie, in an over-sized bow tie, with his face back the way it used to be. 'I told you it wasn't me at the coal house door.'

Robbie was scanning the audience. 'There she is,' Daddy said, and pointed to a small woman, three rows ahead in a turquoise dress with winged shoulder pads. The woman turned and looked up and waved: Mum out in her finery. Neither she nor Robbie looked at me.

'You found them,' I said.

'I did,' Daddy said.

'They look well.' He nodded and smiled. 'Will you leave me alone now?' I asked him.

He looked down at his hands. 'I was right about thawn Thomas boy,' he said. 'He wasn't your match.'

'I won't be told who to love by you,' I said.

'I know.'

I looked around at the packed auditorium, at Mum's shining eyes, back up at him and Robbie. 'I'll see you then,' I said.

I could see his mouth move. 'You know where we are.' He said, and then the song ended, and the audience rose up in applause and blocked my view with their bellowing elbows and the backs of their nodding heads.

The Haggard
P. G. O'Connor

I was thinking one evening would I chance going toward the town, when in comes this auld hag, not a tooth in her head and a huge hape a kids, sayin to me was there any hope of a bite of food to feed their hungry mouths, they hadn't a thing in the house since the father died and the mother went off to England. Bedamn, says I, I've nothing myself except stale bread that I takes off'a the crows down alongside Coffey's public house. I gives it a wipe along the wall, says I, to put a bit of a taste in it, and you're welcome to a bit for yourself and the childer, I've a month's supply saved up in the nitrate sack beyant in the corner. Ah, says she, sure a man like yourself up here all on his own must have the finest of feedin what with all the money I have and she winkin at me.

I seen her givin one of the kids a poke and it starts bawlin and soon the whole hape of them is bawlin and some of them has red hair and more of them has black and more again is blond and at least five or six of every type and shape there is and still th'auld one is croakin at me what about a bit of money and still more comin in the door and not one of them over the age of seven, all screamin and bawlin and pullin flakes of distemper off'a the wall and pullin the papers out of the good chair and they roarin at th'auld hag they were promised sweets. Says th'auld hag what you need is a good woman and hadn't she her hand inside in me pocket but divil the pocket there is there only the family jewels swingin free and by Jaz doesn't she grab a hauld of them and she probably thinking twas a pigskin purse full of money. Well I left a squawk outa me that'd strip a heron but you'd hardly hear it inside in the din that was there that evening and I busted out through the back door into the haggard and away with me through the nettles and briars and over the ditch and away through the slurry tank where the top fell in long ago and down with me into the septic pit and up the other side through the furze bushes where the Conroys have generations of cars stored and down along the face of the quarry and into the swamp, until th'auld hag left go of the family jewels and she sank into the swamp and the children caught up with her and they roarin for sweets.

I staggered back round to the front and opened up the barbed wire gate that I have and up to the front door that hasn't been used in fifty years and sure it came away in me hands. Nothing would do then only for the rain to start tumbling down, so inside I went still holdin the door which I pushed back into the opening. T'was doin this I noticed that there was four legs on the door and sure the way I was after putting it in now weren't the four legs stickin out into the outside and maybe take the eye outa someone's head although no-one had called to the house since I could remember. By Jaz, says I, that's horrid like the table that went missing around the time of the mother's funeral. All the same, says I, better put the legs stickin inwards the way they were, and as soon as I did that didn't I find I was outside again and the rain pourin down on top of me. What harm, says I, isn't the roof inside lakin just as bad sure isn't it nearly all the wan.

So there I was standin in the downpour and along comes a lough of big lumpy men through the bushes. By Jaz, says I, maybe 'tis the county council come to repair the road, sure the main reason I never go anywhere is unless there's no rain for three weeks a fella couldn't tell if he was on the road or not, only that if you went in over your waist in water you were probably strayed off of it. So now seein these lumpy lads and they batin their way through the bushes, I left a roar at them and finally they espied the house about ten feet away and up they come towards me. Well, says I, is there an election on? Damn the election says the big fella and he catches me by the tip of the ear and drags me inside capsizing the table down flat with one kick. We want your money now and be quick about it. Yerra help yourself to all you see, says I, sure I've no need of money here and wouldn't know it if I saw it. Less of the saucy stuff says he and if you don't give up the money right quick you'll be the sorry man. How would that be, says I, curious to know what type of conditions might be worse than the current state of affairs. The other lumpy lads were on for batin me straight away, but after my adventure through the haggard and the slurry and the septic and the swamp, the state of me wasn't the best for layin hands upon, which was why the big fella had caught me by the tip of the ear where the rain probably exposed a bit of skin. They had an auld rope with them and they tied me onto the good chair and they all lookin round for something to bate me with but sure everything was burnt long ago and they could find nothing only maybe to pull apart the good chair and sure wasn't I tied to that. Where's your money roars the big fella or be Jaz I'll... I'll... And he seemed to lose the jist of it. Go on, says I. Have you that pliers Mikey, roars he at one of the lumpy lads, and they still lookin around for money or something to bate me with. Up comes a lad with a rusty auld pliers and gives it to the big fella. I'll pull every tooth of your head he roars. Oh the blessins of God on you sir, says I. Now if he said he was going to pull the hairs outa me nose he'd have had the heart crossways in me, 'cos many's the time I hurt myself sore pullin a block out of the nose and the hairs hangin dearly onto it, but when he came on about the teeth I opened up the gob straightaway so'as he'd get a good swing at the three teeth remaining and they the biggest menace ever, paining me day and night and stopping me chewin the bread, only to soak it in rain and suck at it.

As soon as I opened the gob, sure they wrinkled their noses and screwed up their eyes and turned anyplace else. One of them says maybe we'll pull the fingernails out of him and that'll get him going. Right you are says the big boy and they grab a hauld of me hand and they squintin at it and turning it around, sayin there doesn't seem to be any nails on it. Sure one time I used enjoy biting me nails when I had teeth in me head and nails in me fingers but once th'auld badger ran off with the shovel there was no way of getting the spud only goin at it with the hands and now all the spuds is dug by hand and nary a nail there is on any finger only callouses as thick as the sole of a boot. That one's the thumb says wan'a the lumpy lads, no this one's the thumb says another. But this here's the palm says the first. No it isn't says another, is that his left hand or his right hand? One of the lumpy lads takes a look at me from the side and I suppose what with me trousers being on back to front on account of excessive holes in the knees, and the well'tins on the wrong feet 'cos of a terrible hurry on me back in 1975, and myself looking back over me shoulder to see what were they at, he became horrible confused as to what way round was I at all and sure the poor man fell down in a fit thinking they'd broke me in half putting me into the chair.

What we'll do now, says the big lad, is we'll pull the toenails off of him instead. D'ye hear that, he roars at me, where's the money or we'll pull the toenails off of ya. Small harm to you, says I, and since you've a pliers maybe you'll be able for it and maybe you won't, but myself I haven't been able to get the well'tins off since 1976. Up to that point I used change th'auld sox fairly regular every New Years day. There'd be nothing left of the old ones only the rim and I used pull th'auld rim up the leg to make way for the new sock, then back on with the well'tins pretty quick before I'd suffocate. Only in 1975, what with the thickness of the smell, I closed my eyes and didn't I put the well'tins back on the wrong feet. The following year, I remember it well cos t'was twenty years after the mother died of bad luck from a half-choked magpie, I couldn't get the well'tins off for love nor money neither of which I had, and that was the end of the fresh sox. Be Jaz, says wan of the lumpy men, maybe 'tis inside in the boots he has the money. If it isn't, says the big lad, out with the toenails.

Well, half the lumpy men laid hold of me arms and the rest laid hold of me boots and they went to heaving like a tug-of-war. After half an hour, when I was about six inches longer and nothing else happening, didn't one lad have the idea of heating the boots with fag lighters. They went at it again, yer man full pelt with the fag lighters, and next thing there's a sucking noise and a blue flame and the boots went flyin and the whole place full of the most atrocious stink ever smelt above ground. Bedad 'tis worse than '75, says I to myself, keeping th'auld gob shut for fear of asphyxiation, all the while the lumpy men going purple and boggle-eyed with the stench such as no septic tank ever left loose. In the hope of fresh air, I put the head down and busted out the back door into the haggard and away with me barefoot through the nettles and briars and over the ditch and away through the slurry tank where the top fell in long ago and down with me into the septic pit and up the other side through the furze bushes where the Conroys have generations of cars stored and down along the face of the quarry and into the swamp where there was an awful splashin and screechin and roarin of children and next thing I see th'auld hag and she says There he is and the whole she-bang takes up after me and what with the lumpy men comin behind me I says to myself 'tis into the thicket for me and I running along with stones and sticks and bits of rusty ganvanizing sticking to my feet and sure I thought the smell was catching up on me but wasn't it comin from the feet themselves. So for the pure love of life I bate through the whitethorn thicket and off into th'auld stream and after enough of stones had stuck to me feet and fell off again weren't me feet back to their normal size at least, so I circled back to th'auld cabin to see could I get the well'tins on again right way round this time and maybe risk a breath of air.

I sat down in the chair, trying to pull on the well'tins without taking a breath and listening to the faraway sounds of roarin and screechin in the thicket beyant, and bedad no sooner had I the well'tins on and takin a good suck of air and realizin I was after missing the chance of putting on fresh sox if only I had them, when in over the flattened table comes a dapper man with a beady eye and says he to me do you not know me, I'm your long gone father, back from America. Begob, says I, you're hauldin it better than I am, cos the only hair I have on me head is in me nose and ears and sure yourself has hardly even a bit of grey. Ah 'tis the good life, says he, and hardly was the words out of his mouth than in through the back door is another beady-eyed fella who says I'm yer long gone father, and while them two is takin at one another, in comes another wan and another wan, and next thing they seemed to be comin in the window or down the chimney cos I could hardly see the wall with them and each of them waltzin in and out whispering is there the loan of a few bob to get a business going or thaw out a bank account or pay a ransom and other such things and they had the eyes going round in me head and me with no father at all my whole life and now about fifteen of them of all ages. I was wonderin did the mother fall asleep naked in the dressin room of a hurling match or how did it happen I'd so many fathers, and distraught I was at the memory of years toiling away with no father at all and the mother sitting gobsmacked inside in the chimney, probably broken hearted at the fifteen men who loved her and went to America.

Perplexed with the sorrow of it all, I espied a hole in the wall that I thought I might lep through to get outside but sure wasn't it only a patch of rising damp and didn't I dive headlong at the wall instead of through a hole, poleaxing meself entirely and falling in a fuddle on the floor. Give him air says wan. Give him water says another. Give him room says a third. Give him here says the last. I woke up in a coma, across the back of this lad and he batin across the haggard and away through the nettles and briars and over the ditch and off through the slurry tank where the top fell in long ago and down into the septic pit and up the other side through the furze bushes where the Conroys have generations of cars stored and down along the face of the quarry and through the swamp and into the thicket where there was raucous row and ruille-buille and th'auld hag with a well-aimed stick brings down the father that's carryin me and the rest of them following is tearin at each other and batin into the lumpy men with the horde of children entangled in their legs and biting their knees. Luckily for me being on the ground and being the same colour as the mud itself they couldn't see me at all, so away with me slitherin back the way I came, over ditches and dykes and through all manner of filth and rot towards the haven of my quiet little cabin.

Not far I got however, cos up through the haggard comes all the fathers and the lumpy men and the hag with her screechin children, and I was only up on the mound that used to be the pigsty when I seen a tidy fella comin in through the barbed wire gate, careful-like, and he in a fancy suit and half-spectacles and carrying a tidy little suitcase. I knew he must be the most awful ever cos the whole lot behind me were suddenly quiet save the odd clap agin a child's ear. See gee shees wrong a hane, says th'auld hag and she putting a full set of teeth into her mouth, and says a lumpy lad to one of the fathers Is that you, Father Considine. Tis Sergeant, whispers he, what are you doing here.

Up comes the tidy man to the top of the pigsty and the whole lot of them gathers around. Says he, would you be the man known as Dan Dinny Anne. Deed I am, says I. At long last, says he. If you will sign here I will give you a cheque for one hundred and forty seven million euros, for you have won the lottery. Well, says I, that is an amazing fact. It is, says he. Specially, says I, since I never bought a ticket. What's that, says he, and he cross as a wasp. Aren't you Dan Dinny Anne, known as Dan Dinny Anne the Bog? No says I, I'm Dan Dinny Anne the Haggard, Dan Dinny Anne the Bog lives beyant in the swamp.

Well by Jaz I was thrun upside down by the stampede. When t'was over there was only myself and the tidy man left above on the pigsty. He looked down at me a moment and with a small sigh he starts pickin his way back to the barbed wire gate. Good riddance, says I, and went in to sit down on the good chair and damn the goin to town.

Woman Cubed
Laura Rock

The spells began as Dale was preparing for her breakthrough performance and also worrying about running into that man. For almost a year he'd been surprising her with pretty trifles left at the door—French soaps in the form of shooting stars; Belgian chocolate trapeze artists swinging across an edible tableau; a German doll that would dance with a few turns of the key in her back. As the company's prima contortionist, Dale was accustomed to receiving flowers, of course – on average, half a dozen men ordered roses in the afterglow of her intimate, impossible shows, each thinking himself a romantic genius – but the rabid fan sent African violets, one pot at a time.

Every delivery claimed space on the windowsill and added new colour to the white apartment, where nothing had lived with Dale and Derek before now. The plants reminded Dale of her mother. She had filled their house with greenery, mostly big-leaf tropicals, light-hogs vying for the windows. As a young girl, Dale observed the outside world through perpetually dewy glass; it was like growing up inside a terrarium. Cradling an offering of *Saintpaulia inconspicua,* she inhaled the smell of dank earth and was home.

About the special performance, Dale had been told two nights ago that recruiters from the Cirque – *that* Cirque, top of the top – would be coming to watch her. Insiders, people who no longer took calls from Derek but still liked her, whispered this news in her ear while she sat for dress-rehearsal makeup. Dale turned her head in surprise, and the bustling stage-set tilted. Sound crews, spotlights, ropes slung in braids, and the costume lady pushing her rack of clothes all slipped sideways. Dale's vision cleared almost immediately, but her nervous system had been whirring and beeping ever since.

Derek made soothing teas and drew bubble-baths, but she refused to relax. There was so much to do. It wasn't enough that she could fold herself like origami and squeeze into a clear acrylic cube not much bigger than carry-on luggage. She couldn't rely on her storied ability to dislocate shoulders and hips at will. A snake unhinges its jaw in order to consume larger prey, but that doesn't make it anything more than a mildly interesting freak. No, she needed to rebuild her act completely, starting with the brand.

Dale ran through new stage names as if testing ring-tones. 'Clarissa LaRose', the persona she'd adopted when Derek discovered her as a teenaged gymnast, was so over.

"Mi-mi-mi Mirandella, Mirella," Dale sang, trilling her r's.

She stood on one foot and pulled the other over her head. In her flesh-coloured unitard, she was a living anatomy lesson. Not one centimetre of her body was soft, yet she had the gift of making bones dissolve. Her malleability was a kind of softness.

"La-la-la Lacrimosa, Milagrosa—no, that sounds fat."

Derek scribbled on a notepad. His graying shoulder-length curls bobbed as he jiggled his crossed leg.

"What's wrong with the status quo?" He said. "Ditch Clarissa, you've got zero name recognition. I'm fond of Clarissa."

"Just fond? Not *in love with*?" Dale shook her ponytail at him, which caused the room to wobble. She dropped her foot and everything settled, but it felt temporary. Could the problem be the azure-tinted contacts she'd just purchased? She was tired of plain brown eyes and much preferred the startling intensity of her new irises. "This is the last possible moment to change. Once I'm in the big leagues, it's too late. Sorpresa, Spiritessa," she said, "La Vida, La Viva, La Veda—"

"Dale," Derek murmured. He moved behind her, rubbing her shoulders.

"What?" Dale leaned into his teddy-bear torso and tipped her head back, then wished she hadn't. She gripped his arms around her waist until the dizziness passed.

"*Dale.* What about Dale?"

"Totally inappropriate." She stepped clear of him. "Even you can see that." Dale didn't mean to snap—so unlike the early days, when she was Derek's adoring puppet-in-a-box. But what a pain he'd been lately, arguing about every clause in her contracts, alienating executives who only wanted more of her. He said, "I'm protecting your interests," as if the company was some kind of enemy. "Trust me," he said.

Derek pointed both index fingers at her, thumbs up. "It's the name your mother gave you. I'm just saying."

Dale touched the vial that dangled from her necklace. She wore it at all times except during shows, when the relic ashes of her mother posed a lethal hazard. She strived for a case-closed tone. "Mama understands that I have to change my name. An artist knows, in here," she said, tapping her chest.

"Oh, artists. The artists I've dealt with." Derek shrugged. "Okay, you win. You and Mama Grow-op."

"Please. Like your mother can be tolerated for a single hour." Dale moved to the window and watered each pot, taking her time.

"Let's not start that again," Derek said. "Mother didn't mean to insult you by bringing her own dinner—"

"I just think you should count your blessings. Lots of men would appreciate a dead mother-in-law."

"If only she'd stay out of our creative decisions." Derek cleared his throat. "Something else. Your friend again."

"My number one fan?" Dale spun around and regretted her haste. She clutched her neck.

"I've informed the cops. Once more, they do nothing."

"Is devotion such a crime?"

When the notes first started coming, Derek reported a stalker to the authorities, and they proposed a sting. Law enforcement would catch the guy in the act, some act of adoration.

"If you people think that I'd allow my wife, a performer of the highest calibre who will soon be famous worldwide, to be used as bait, forget it," Derek had said. "What happened to old-fashioned police work? Ever hear of that?" He threw the phone on the floor.

Dale had been stretching, preparing to enter her practice cube. She jackknifed into a fluid pike-press headstand. At times like this, Derek made more sense upside-down. "Do you think it's wise," she said, bicycling her legs, "to hang up on the cops? They also know where we live."

Now, spread out on the floor again, Dale wished she could just rehearse. The cube was in the corner of the bedroom, empty and gleaming. Calling her to come inside and disappear. Sometimes Dale had the sensation of splitting into facets: the single-jointed woman whose body took up the usual amount of space; the compressed woman imprinting the cube with her skin cells; and the spirit-woman floating above the spectacle, formless and free, able to see what the audience sees and report back. All three simultaneously. Not always, but at the best, highest moments of her art, it happened.

"What did he say this time?" Dale pushed her spine into the floorboards.

"Same old."

"Read it." She visualized the performance she'd need to win the Cirque: transcendent, personal best.

"Nope. No way."

"Read, Derek." Triumphant. Her star discovered again, but bigger. "Darling."

"I've thrown it away. It's gone." Derek waved his hand in the air. He tied an apron around his middle, picked up a dust cloth and began to wipe the windowsill, rattling pots as he moved them.

"Careful with my violets! Come on, you keep ten-year old gas receipts."

Derek pulled a page of cream vellum from his pocket and unfolded it, sighing. "I offer the answers you seek."

"Hmm. And?"

"Your latest problem is a sign, he says. Sign of what, exactly? Such crap."

"What else?"

"Undying love." Derek reddened. "The mystery man confesses love, how original."

"See, some people appreciate artists. Give me," she said, holding out her hand.

"No, I don't think—"

"I want it."

"What's the attraction here? You have trainers. You have a manager, me."

"Don't forget husband," Dale said.

"Funny. Stay away from this guy—I mean it."

"It's not like I'm meeting him secretly. I don't even know who he is." Dale's words turned cartwheels around her cranium, rapid revolutions of light.

"Freaking nutcase," Derek said, dusting the coffee table. "He shows up here, I'm throwing him down the stairs."

Dale puffed her cheeks, panting. "Never mind. What's *wrong* with me?"

Hours later, Dale lay in bed fighting nausea as Derek phoned the company doctor, physiotherapist, chiropractor, and psychic in turn. How unfair: her big moment finally here, and she couldn't imagine slithering through a tight maze of pipe, making crowds gasp, nor hanging by her hair from a chain as children screamed. All she could do was stay still, suffering the bed spins of a common drunk.

Without even examining her, the doctor diagnosed benign paroxysmal positional vertigo. "There's nothing benign about it," Dale said to the ceiling. Paroxysmal was a mystery, but positional she understood. Who knew positions better? And vertigo—a balance disorder, causes murk. No one could explain why nerve-dwelling crystals of the inner ear would suddenly decide to migrate into the semicircular canals, leaving Dale reeling as they fled their ancestral homeland. Derek sat by her bedside and briefed her on uncertain cures: drugs, acupuncture, spinal adjustments, yogic manipulations of the head and more.

"The doctor called in a prescription. You'll be normal in no time."

"Will that work? What did the psychic say? The show's the day after tomorrow." Dale yelled, "I should be practising."

"The truth? You're not performing. It pains me – huge opportunity, don't think I don't know what this means to you – to us. But." He patted the quilt around her. "I'll speak to the honchos-that-be about getting another audition. I've still got connections at the Cirque. I can make that happen."

Dale moaned. "There has to be something. Herbs, crystals, homeowhatever." She reached for his hand, hitting it. "Go. Out. And. Find. Me. Something."

"But—"

"Now!"

Dale drifted into thin sleep, recalling everything the fan had ever written to her. At first she found it creepy that he knew so much, like future performances that hadn't been announced yet. But the gifts piled up, no harm done. Over time, the guy began to seem *benign.* Like a super-active guardian angel. When she made some small change to her act, she found herself waiting for his reaction. He always noticed; his letters critiqued every new move.

Once he wrote, "Stagecraft is a calling to destroy limitations. Hold your position five beats longer than you think you can. Subject the audience to your will. Release them with reluctance."

"Hocus-pocus," Derek had said, adding that note to his collection.

At the time, Dale was coiled in her own limbs. Her voice began to waver as she entered the floating stage of practice. "I did try that one thing he suggested, craning my neck a degree counterintuitively, and you know what?" She beamed in Derek's direction. "It worked."

Dale moved through the splits before entering the cube.

"Dale? Don't listen to him. Hear me?"

She stared through the clear wall, nose smushed, lips distended.

At dusk, still in bed and waiting for Derek to return with the treatments, Dale's mother blew into her head. Since Mama's death, these fleeting appearances were all Dale had. It was a chance to ask questions, such as, Why the blah name? Were you depressed when I was born? What did you imagine my future would be? Dale wondered if she was living up to maternal expectations. Specifically, whether Mama was pleased with contortions as a line of work, and what she thought of Derek. Mama might appreciate Derek's nurturing side, but she was also quick to see a man's faults and prescribe harsh treatment, much as she might tackle an aphid infestation. Vertiginous, immobile, Dale heard Mama's pronouncements all too clearly: he's too old for you, his best days in the business are behind him, and he's no joy to look at—move on. "After the big show," Dale promised, half asleep. "Soon."

Dale woke not knowing the day or time. The doorbell had rung, she remembered. She thought that the physio who made house calls must have let himself in, but the man standing before her – tall, forbidding, angular

– was a stranger. He took off his black fedora. His eyes fixed her in a cat-like green beam—real or contacts? She smiled, dazed. When he spoke, she heard bubbles in liquid. He might have said, "Your mother sent me." She hoped so.

The man helped Dale into her favourite position. He rolled her over so she was face down, then coached her into a backfold: legs curled up and over the head, feet planted in front of ears; pelvis stacked on head; chin in hands. Her abdominal muscles pulled taut, grounding her. She was a spider on the web, contemplative and wise. She could stay like this forever.

Heavy footsteps trudged up the stairs. Derek flung the door open. His voice barely reached her.

"I've got your medicine," he called from the hallway. He entered the bedroom and stopped. "What the—? What's he—?"

The man ignored Derek, bending down to whisper in Dale's ear. He showed her a sprinkling of lavender pills, tiny pellets in his palm.
"Extract of *saintpaulia* and other necessaries. Highly potent ingredients," he said.

Dale didn't move; she was stable and relaxed.

Derek rattled a paper bag. "*This* is your prescription. I've got it here."

The man stood up and stared at Derek, who retreated to the hallway.

"Snap out of it Dale. Don't take anything from him." Derek backed away further.

The man stroked Dale's throat. "Now," he said. She opened her mouth. He fed her the pills and closed her jaw. "Good girl."

"You were nothing before I found you," Derek shouted from somewhere in the apartment. "Your mother raised plants, and dick-all for you; *I* was the one who honed your talent."

The man gently helped Dale untangle and walked her to the cube. He held her hand as she slid inside.

"It's over," Derek yelled. He picked up a violet and threw it. The pot smashed, dirt exploding on white wall. "You're finished. Who ever heard of a dizzy contortionist?"

Dale moulded herself to the cube's surface, angling her head downward. She felt fine. No spins, no spells.

Another pot crashed, then silence.

"Float on the surface of skewed perception," the man said. "Don't succumb to distraction's undertow."

Peace. Dale was the space available, no more, no less. The strictures of the cube fit perfectly.

"Give the performance of your life," the man said, tracing her face lovingly. He put his hat on and walked to the door, then turned back. "One more thing. From now on, you are La Reina Anguila."

"Queen Something," Dale said, or tried to say—her lips were stuck to the cube, yet he heard.

"Eel." The man tipped his brim and walked out, leaving her alone.

"Yes, La Reina Anguila," she breathed. "Just right."

Sophie Hampton
White Socks and Weirdos

'Hey, Weirdo. Why do you wear spaz clothes?' says Lorraine Abbot at playtime, hands on hips. She stares at my woolly tights and Clarks shoes, her eyes as dark and narrow as the coin slot on our gas meter. My legs itch and burn as though she's put a curse on them.

Are you deaf *and* dumb?' she says.

My face goes the colour of Mum's lipstick. I know what the colour feels like because when Lorraine makes my cheeks hot and my heart B-BOOM, B-BOOM, I go to the girls' toilets: two plums in the mirror.

'My mum buys them,' I say.

'Tights are for spastics,' says popular Lorraine in knee-high white socks and patent shoes. On Monday, her eighth birthday, she was the first girl in my class to walk to school on her own. She showed off about it All Day Long. On Tuesday she came into the classroom at twenty to ten, with puffy frog eyes and her mum; big boys on bikes had chased her and she had run back home and cried. The Witches had crowded round and made stupid noises. By afternoon register, the big boys had turned into men wearing balaclavas.

'I'm allowed to choose my own clothes,' Lorraine says. She flicks back her long hair cut straight at the ends. 'Skip with us.' She pushes me into the middle of the Witches.

Ooh, ahh, I lost my bra. I left my knickers in my boyfriend's car! they chant as the skipping rope twirls faster and faster under my feet. I know they're going to trip me up so I hope they do it soon; the waistband on my tights has lost its grippiness and the tights will slither down my skinny legs, sticky-out knee bits round my ankles.

The girls jerk the rope and when I fall everybody laughs. I graze my palms: red scratches, grey dust, yellow gunk.

'Why don't you ever invite anyone to tea?' asks Lorraine. 'Is it because you live in a gippo caravan?'

I don't invite anyone for tea because our flat is embarrassing. Nobody I know lives anywhere like me, in a block in King's Cross where people throw rubbish into the yard from their windows at night and the corridor walls are stained yellow with wee. Lorraine and the Witches live in the new estate on the edge of the park.

Other things are embarrassing too. Last Christmas, Mum made leaflets about being vegetarian: *Meat is Murder* she wrote and *No Blood on My Hands.* Nathan, my brother, and I drew pigs and cows and splodges of red paint on the sheets of paper. Mum took the leaflets, and us, round all the local butchers and all the local butchers told her to *fuck off.* She was brave: butchers are scary what with their stained-brown aprons and sharp knives. Their shops smelt like the taste when I nibble my nails after I've been on the rusty swings in the rec.

On Saturday mornings, when everyone else in my class watches *Multi-Coloured Swap Shop,* Mum and I take the washing to the launderette in black plastic sacks. I worry that the bags will split and our jumble sale clothes will spill onto the pavement. I have to carry my sack with both hands so I can't pull up my tights or scratch the eczema on the insides of my knees.

'Weirdo, don't ignore me. I said why don't you invite anyone to tea?' Lorraine gives me a dark and narrow look.

B-BOOM, B-BOOM. I want to slot two pence pieces into her eyes, push them into her brain. Who'd be the spaz then? She dangles the skipping rope from the middle and the handles knock together: click, click, click, click. She swings the rope and the handles whizz round in a blur, like a spinning top. When she flicks the skipping rope into my tummy, quick and hard, I bend over a bit. A sound pushes out. Like an animal.

'Sit with us at dinner time,' orders Lorraine as I walk away. 'Or – you're – DEAD.'

Two plums in the mirror. I press one cheek and then the other against the cold tiles. It's four hours and forty-five minutes until the end of term, thank God. I hate Lorraine and the Witches, the way they call me *Dork* or *Weirdo* or once, when I dared to answer back, *F-ing Flid*. I hate my black tights and wonky Mum cut fringe and posh voice and not being able to say who I fancy on *Top of the Pops* or *Grange Hill* because we don't have a television.

The milk I drank at playtime bubbles into my mouth and I spit it into the sink. I turn on the tap, whoooosh, and close my eyes and shoot Lorraine Abbot through the head.

At lunchtime I sit on a toilet seat for an hour and nobody tries the door. Five bits of the graffiti on the walls are about me. The worst says WEIRDIE WEIRDO. The letters are black except for the DIE which is red. I spit on a piece of toilet roll and rub at the letters but they don't even smudge. When I stand up, white lights dance in front of my eyes. I rub the pins and needles in my legs as I hop from one foot to the other.

Mum picks me up after school. She is wearing too short shorts cut from jeans and a vest top which says *Give Peas a Chance*. Curly hairs grow out of her armpits. I glance round to make sure the Witches aren't in the playground; Lorraine's mum is wearing a blouse and skirt.

'Come *on*, Mummy,' I say, walking as fast as I can. Mum's clogs clip-clop on the pavement. Once we turn the corner I slow down.

'What did you have for lunch?' asks Mum.

'Nothing,' I say. 'Wasn't hungry.' I start to cry. Mum holds my hand and the graze stings. I tell her some of what happened in the playground and why I was too scared to eat.

She digs some rice cakes out of her bag. 'I'm going to speak to Miss Harvey after the holidays. Lorraine Abbot is a bully.'

'No! You can't. Lorraine'll kill me.'

'You'll kill yourself if you don't eat.'

'I could take packed lunches. Children who take packed lunches eat in a different room. Please, Mum.'

'Okay. It will be easier for you to be vegetarian. Have another rice cake.'

We're in the launderette, watching our clothes in the tumble dryer. The zips and buttons clunk and thud as they roll around the drum. I have picked the bobbles off the tights I'm wearing and made a pile of fluff on the magazine table.

'Mummy?'

'Yes?'

I take a breath of warm air, full of the clean smell of washing. 'Please will you buy me some white socks for school?'

'Why?'

'Because all the other girls wear white socks.'

'No.'

'Why not?'

'Because it's not about what the other girls wear. It's hard to keep socks white and hot washes are bad for the environment. Anyway, you've got plenty of tights.'

I want to curl up in a washing machine and go round and round.

'But Mummy ... '

'No.'

My chin drops onto my chest. My blue shoes are sprinkled with soap powder. Like stars.

The week before the start of term, on Child Allowance day, Mum comes back from the shops with a pair of long white socks. I squeal and hug her. The socks have diamond shapes made from holes and the elastic is strong and grips my legs even when I jump up and down in front of the mirror.

On the last day of the holidays, I lay out my clothes on a chair. If I have packed lunches and wear socks things might not be so bad. And even though I only have one pair, I'll wash them every night – Get your whites right it says on the powder box – and wear them every day. Lorraine will never be able to say that I wear spazza tights again.

'Lorraine Abbot?'

Silence.

'Lorraine Abbot?'

There is no *Yes, Miss* when Miss Harvey calls the register. Darren who lives next door to Lorraine says her mum kept her home because she's got a sore throat. I hope that she'll come in after lunch and notice my socks and think that I'm not-weird. When the bell goes at quarter past three, I'm embarrassed that I've spent days imagining the moment when Lorraine will see my socks.

I wash them when I get home, squeeze them hard and sprain my wrist. After supper, Nathan and I help Dad paint the CND sign onto an old sheet. Nathan draws a circle with black paint and I do the headless three-legged hangman in the middle. Mum has the neatest writing so she does the letters. Dad takes the brush off the broom and uses the handle to make a flag pole.

'What's this for?' I ask.

'Wait and see,' says Dad.

My socks are still damp in the morning and Mum won't let me dry them with the hair dryer; she's cross because we're late for school. I wear my tights but the funny thing is, Lorraine doesn't even notice.

'Hey, Weirdo! Why are you wearing flid shoes?'

B-BOOM, B-BOOM.

I go to the fourth year classroom to eat my lunch. My sandwich is wrapped in a paper bag which has grease stains on it. I peel apart thick slices of brown bread: Mum has mashed up boiled eggs. There is a chunk missing from each slice, where the loaf stuck to the tin.

'Your food stinks,' says Dwayne as he bites into his sandwich; pale ham, thin as a cat's tongue, flops over the edge of his white bread.

'Yuck. Go and pong somewhere else,' says Warren. 'Go *on!*'

I move to a corner of the room. One, two, three, four round pieces of gum, pink and grey, cling like snails to the edge of the table. I look down at my shoes and a tear drops on the buckle and trickles onto the floor. Mum will never buy me black patents. Never in a million years.

I take a bite of my sandwich: a crunch of eggshell in my ears, a glossy lump of margarine on my tongue. For a few seconds, the ball of half-chewed crust sticks in my throat and won't go down or come up.

We don't go back to our flat after school. We meet up with some of Mum and Dad's friends and go to a beautiful white house near Coram's Fields. I recognise the area because Nathan and I played in the park when we were little. Little enough to splash in the paddling pool, me in just my knickers and him in nothing at all.

The house has steps and pillars either side of a black front door. When the door opens I feel like Alice in Wonderland: O mouth and double O eyes. The house is full of sunshine and cream carpets and shiny metal furniture and leather sofas and rubber plants taller than Dad.

I count fourteen rooms and Nathan counts fifteen but we are too excited to argue. Mum says we will live here for a bit and I have never been so happy in All My Life. Dad opens one of the upstairs windows and hangs out the CND flag; the D has dribbled so it looks like a P. The grown-ups cook huge saucepans of lentil soup and buckwheat while the children play hide-and-seek.

I open the door to what must be a little girl's room. Everything's pink and floaty, except for an Evel Knievel set on the floor. There's a photo of a girl wearing a school uniform: burgundy jumper and skirt, checked shirt, straw hat with a ribbon. Tights. It doesn't look like she gets called Weirdo because she's smiling.

Ready or not I'm coming to get you! yells a boy called River. I step into a wardrobe and click the door shut. It smells posh inside, of lavender; the wardrobe at home smells of cheesy feet. I stroke a velvety dress and a silky one and wonder if I dare to try them on. When River comes into the room, I hide behind the clothes. I don't think he would have found me if I hadn't got the giggles.

I sleep in a bed which is so soft it feels like there's nothing underneath me, even my bony bits. I dream that Lorraine comes to tea. *Your house is beautiful, she says. Please be my friend. Cross your heart and hope to die, stick a needle in my eye.* And I do. Right through the black bit in the middle.

I sit up. My heart B-BOOMS fast and I can hardly breathe. I'm in a car and it's dark except for blue flashing lights. A strange man is sitting in the front seat and someone has their arms round me.

'Mummy!' I scream and realise that I have been asleep on her knee. I burst into tears and she tightens her grip. Egg sick in my nose.

'I can't believe you slept through it,' she says, as she wipes my face with her sleeve. She explains that we are in a police car and have been arrested for squatting a rich man's house. She says that she and Dad and their friends don't think it's right that people own second homes they hardly use when others, like us, are so poor. I don't think it's right either. It's weird being poor and living in the depressing flat in King's Cross but it's also weird to wake up in a police car.

It's light the next time I open my eyes. I'm in my own bed with its lumps and uncomfortable springs. Mum and Dad and Nathan are talking in the kitchen. It's good that we're not in prison but it's sad that we didn't stay in the big house long enough to invite Lorraine for tea.

Mum comes into the bedroom. 'Everything's okay,' she says. 'You don't have to go to school today, the local paper wants to interview us. We're going to have our photo taken.'

Everything is exciting again. I wear the flowery tunic that I've been saving for a special occasion. Mum bought it in a jumble sale but it's brand new, it still has the label on. I pull on my socks and peer in the mirror: my fringe is definitely wonky so I pin it back with the kirby grip I found in the street.

The photographer is waiting in the concrete recreation ground opposite our block, with the other people who squatted the house. He arranges the adults at the back and the children at the front, except for Nathan who runs off. The photographer doesn't say *smile* or *cheese* like photographers usually do, he tells us to look angry.

After the photos and interviews, everyone heads off to their poor homes. Mum discovers that Nathan is chewing gum; he must have peeled it off the pavement. He does that. He clutches a syringe and refuses to let go. Mum goes mental: she says that she hates living in London. When we get home she puts Nathan in the bath, even though there's no hot water, and makes him gargle with Dettol.

Dad says he'll buy two copies of the paper the next day, so that I can take one to school. I plan to cut out the photo and leave the writing bit at home because I don't think Lorraine will understand squatting. She would think it was even weirder than wearing tights and Clarks on hot days. But if I cut out the photo, Lorraine will see that I have been in the paper and notice my tunic and socks.

When I wake up, Dad has already been to the shop on the corner. I jump out of bed but my heart b-booms when I see the photo. It's only little and it's black and white of course so you can't tell that my tunic is orange and flowery and you can hardly make out my face. When I hold the paper close-up, the picture goes dotty and hurts my eyes. The worst thing is that the photographer has cut everyone off at the waist so I may as well have been wearing tights and nobody, not even Lorraine, would have known.

So I don't take the photo to school. I spend ages getting ready though and put on my tunic and socks and pin back my fringe. I walk behind Mum and avoid the pavement cracks which means that Lorraine will be in.

The pavement cracks are wrong. Lorraine isn't in.

'Quiet everybody,' says Miss Harvey after lunch. 'Lorraine Abbot was knocked over by a car this morning. She ran across a road because those big boys on bikes chased her again. She was taken to University College Hospital.'

Please let her be dead. Please say she was declared dead on arrival like they do on the radio.

'Thankfully she's had a very lucky escape. She's got a broken leg and a couple of cracked ribs but the doctors are amazed that she wasn't killed. She's already sitting up eating jelly and ice cream.'

Oohs and ahhs and sniffs and Witches' arms flung round each others' shoulders.

Lucky Lorraine it says under the photo in the paper a few days later. It's on the front page. You can see that she's wearing her long white socks.

The Café at the V&A
Thomas Watson

The café at the museum was crowded, even for a Friday night, with animated office workers and louche artistes hunkered over white circular tables, cherry picking stories from their respective weeks. Roger sat with his back to the room, listening to the chatter from neighbouring tables as he thumbed the patterned swirls engraved upon his silver Zippo. He preferred to eavesdrop on a discussion concerning the geographical imbalances of the labour market rather than contribute to the conversation at his own table that Marie was dominating. A waitress appeared at his shoulder as an unexpected tirade of expletives escaped from the kitchen and tinkled off the decorative Victorian wall tiles like notes from a glockenspiel. "Something else to drink, sir?" she asked.

Roger hooked his elbow over the back of the sculpted plastic chair and twisted in his seat to get a better view of her. "Same again please."

"Manhattan – two cherries – in a tumbler?"

He nodded and watched her until she was lost in the opulent fog of the Gamble Room. The café retained many of the gaudy features from the original Victorian refreshment room and the modern touches in most instances complemented the aesthetic. Only the three oversized orb-shaped chandeliers struck Roger as being out of place—too ethereal against the robust practicality of the marble fireplace at the far end of the room. He pulled a small plastic tobacco pouch from his jacket pocket and turned back to face the group. A dozen of them were crammed round a table set for eight; mostly they were people he knew vaguely or not at all, Marie's friends. Mark and his girlfriend Tess were the exceptions; he still laid claim to them in his mind.

Marie sat across from him, she had decided to wear her silver wig and the hairpiece glinted in the light of the chandeliers. Roger saw that it sat lop-sided and smiled at her crooked fringe as he set to work on his roll up. When they were out just the two of them he would look for the compassioned looks of strangers who failed to realise that his girlfriend suffered from nothing more than what he had begun to call a forced eccentricity.

The waitress returned with the second round of aperitifs. Marie received her champagne without breaking from her conversation. "I'm so happy for you Serge. Happy for you both." She placed a hand on Serge's arm, smiled up at Guillaume, and raised her glass. "Here's to a fabulous engagement—to the most handsome couple in the room. *Salud*."

Roger set his half-rolled cigarette on the table and took up his tumbler as crystal champagne saucers clinked about him. His was the only drink not brimming with bubbles and he enjoyed a long swig. With a toothpick he skewered one of the red cherries and bit down on the gelatinous fruit. The taste of sweet morello tinged with vermouth flooded his mouth as he watched the waitress continue her circuit. Marie took a small tortoise shell disc from her clutch, flipped it open and adjusted her wig in the reflection. "Warhol? Don't get me started on Warhol." She clapped the compact mirror shut like a castanet and placed it beside her soup spoon. "I know he's some kind of hero to you, Marcel, but come on dear, he's so clearly a fuckwit." Murmurs of discontent threatened to disrupt her flow, but Marie talked over them. "Anyone here could take an image, brighten the colour palette and mass produce it until the meme permeates the subconscious and someone has the ludicrosity to call it social commentary. I mean even…" She looked at Roger, thought better of it and returned to her champagne.

Her condemnation provoked a stern response from the table as half a dozen voices jabbered at once—Lucille led the dissent, keen to defend her husband's appreciation of the avant-garde. Roger kept his head bowed and wondered if 'ludicrosity' was a real word. Outwardly, he remained focused on constructing his cigarette: rolling the paper into a cylindrical pipe until it enveloped the leaves within. He moistened the join with his tongue, tapped the bottom twice on the edge of the table and, content the tobacco was evenly packed, tucked the cigarette with the black curls behind his ear.

"Marie, Marie," said Guillaume. "Come on now. What about Sierra?"

"The Spaniard? Tattoos Cubans and calls it art? Overblown."

Serge leaned over and whispered in her ear. "Excuse Guillaume, he's just back from Berlin. Took a peek at the Boros collection while he was there. Obsessed with the man."

Guillaume continued in his heavily accented English. "All he does these days is make little models of his art, then he gets his little tinkerbells to run round cities with the oversized versions. They do the heavy lifting. To me, these days, he is the greatest. And to him, the art, it is just the idea."

Marie shook her head. "Art is more than that."

"Is it?" asked Guillaume. "If you believe that, then maybe this is not the business for you." He drank from his wide-rimmed glass.

"It has to be more than the idea alone, more than a concept. As artists, we have to execute as well. Otherwise… " Marie looked at her champagne saucer; it was nearly empty.

"Otherwise what?"

"Look. Artists are not CEOs, or middle managers—delegating should not come in to it."

"Tell that to Michelangelo," said Serge. "The Sistine Chapel is not the achievement of one man. No, he had assistants mixing the paint, running the ladders—and I tell you… "

"I tell you Serge; in that case, he's a fuckwit too."

Roger looked up and reread the line from Ecclesiastes inscribed high in the decorative frieze: 'There is nothing better for a man than that he should eat and drink, and make his soul enjoy the good of his labour.' Too right, he thought, and taking up the heavy bottomed tumbler he finished his drink.

Behind him the waitresses milled about the overspill of seated customers, slaloming between the four iconic columns that dominated the room. They moved with an efficiency that echoed the simplicity of their outfits: black ties on white shirts, black skirts and spotless aprons; their shoes pattered across the burnt red earthenware floor as they brought out the starters. Roger considered his ham hock terrine and wished he'd gone for the red onion tart. Across from him Marie reached for a bread roll, bangles jangling on her arms.

"God, autumn menus in this town are so very depressing," she said as she seasoned her soup. "If there was a blight on butternut squash there would be pandemonium in kitchens from Goodge Street to Portobello." She reached for the pepper.

"At least it's not Campbell's." Roger said, after a pause.

A hush descended around the table.

"What was that, Roger? Something to say?" Marie's eyes, sticky with thick lines of makeup, swallowed him like quicksand.

"I said: *least it's not Campbell's...* "

"Oh Roger, Roger, how witty. You truly are a proponent of bons mots." She clapped her hands together. "Congratulations on overcoming *l'esprit de l'escalier,*" she continued. "You know darling, you are wasted in admin. Table, another toast: to our dear Roger—the Cream of Warhol." Marie looked about at the fellow diners and raised her glass. Serge looked at Guillaume. Guillaume looked at Tess. Tess looked at Mark who made sure to look at nobody.

Roger held her stare, reading the diagonal cuts in the tumbler with the tips of his fingers. Marie clinked her champagne saucer with Lucille and took a sip. Setting her glass back on the table, she brushed a hand across her cheek, freeing a couple of stray synthetic hairs that had caught in the corner of her mouth. Roger noted a small glob of orange soup clumped around the tip of one of the silver strands. Turning to Mark, he took the silver lighter from beside his steak knife, flipped back the lid and sparked the flint twice.

"Cigarette?" he asked.

Mark nodded in confirmation and chewed on a mouthful of onion tart. "Be right behind you."

Roger's footfalls echoed back at him from all sides of the quad as he skirted the leftover puddles from an earlier downpour and headed away from the glow of the refreshment rooms. The late autumnal chill was severe and he lifted the collar of his blazer for warmth as a soft drizzle fell. Along the wall, a narrow rain shadow formed where the balustrade created a slight overhang. He leaned against the dry red brick, wedged the cigarette in the corner of his mouth and lit it. Exhaling slowly, a steady stream of blue smoke muddled the damp air. In the middle of the garden the oval water feature was all but empty and had the forgotten look of a shallow paddling pool in winter.

Mark emerged through the double doors and spotted Roger down the terrace. He walked over and removed a cigarette from a pack of Camels. "Miserable night, eh," he said.

Roger nodded and handed Mark his Zippo. He drew a deep breath and watched the tip of his cigarette flare against the clouds above—themselves tinged with the orange of streetlamps from Exhibition Road.

"What's with Marie?" Mark spun the wheel against the flint; the spurt of flame distorted the shadows on his face as he raised the light. "Everything alright?"

"Not exactly." Roger took another drag and shook his head. "We're calling time. Six years. Time to tap out." He looked in to the middle distance.

"Holy cow. And Canada?"

"Not going to happen. Well for her at least. Doesn't seem to be much point heading off to build a new life together when she's shagging around here."

"Damn…mate." Mark looked at the floor and scraped the soles of his shoes across the Italian paving. "Any idea of the, er, bedfellow?"

"Lautrec—I think."

"Lautrec?" Mark shuffled his weight on to his left foot and cocked his head, studying Roger's face. "You sure?"

"It's got to be. And if it's not him… well, she's definitely getting her bread buttered at some other table."

"Damn." Mark blew smoke upwards in to the air.

"I mean, he's all she ever talks about. It's all *Lautrec thinks this and Lautrec said that.* Hell if I care, but if that's not swooning, I don't know what is." Roger flicked ash in to the gutter. "You know she's been spending more and more time at the gallery? Tess mention that to you? He asked to see her portfolio about a month back, which by the way is round about the time we last fucked. He's building her up, filling her head with bullshit ideas, telling her to keep painting, to stay in London." Roger shook his head, dragged on his cigarette. "It's a total line and she's paying out for it."

Mark drew a lung-load of smoke and shrugged. "Tess mentioned he's a bit of a sex pest. Nothing explicit, just always comes across as a bit of a creep. You know, he reminds me a little of Brando in *Last Tango in Paris*. Fatter and pervier, though. Bigger nose, as well." He tapped Roger's arm with the back of his hand. "Hey, you don't think he's been asking her to '*pass zee butter*'?"

Roger moved his arm away. "Thanks for the image."

"Ah c'mon Rog. If you want a sympathetic ear, you'd be talking to your priest, your mother or the Samaritans, so don't play that card." He cupped his hands together and blew hot breath in to the air pocket. "This is a good thing. I mean, better you find out now, than a year down the line, knee deep in snow and misery in B.C. Don't waste your time moping. Move along."

"Gee Mark, you're a regular fucking 8-ball."

"Yeah. Well... " Mark shrugged and pulled his arms tighter across his chest. "Anyway, isn't he supposed to be here?"

"Running late I guess."

"You going to say anything?"

"You sound like Marie. Don't worry, I'm not going to ruin the night for Serge and Guillaume. Tempted to slash the tyres on his Jag, but I figure that can wait a week."

Mark nodded. "Good lad."

On the opposite side of the quad a kitchen porter emerged through a side door, casting light across the garden. He sat in silhouette on an upturned yellow mixer crate and removed his cap.

Roger lowered his voice and went on. "Three fucking years we've been planning this move and now she wants to go off and find herself like bloody Pocahontas or something." He tossed the stub of the rollup into a plant pot.

"Mate, you've got your analogy all wrong there." Mark waved the tip of his cigarette in the air as he spoke, jabbing at the half-light. "Pocahontas was wild from the get go—it was only when she was seduced by Captain Smith and his wily colonial mercantilism that she shunned her tree hugging ways."

Roger looked up at him from under a raised eyebrow.

"You're welcome to borrow the DVD anytime."

"Give me one of those, will you."

Mark took the Camels from his shirt pocket and shook the box lightly until one of the filters broke ranks. Roger removed it from the carton and stuck it in the corner of his mouth. He patted down his pockets. "You got that light?"

Mark took the Zippo from his trouser pocket and raised the flame, holding it steady as his friend drew in the heat until the tobacco caught. He snapped the lid shut with his thumb and offered the lighter back to Roger. "Nice lighter," he said. "Careful, or I'll run off with it."

"Keep it. It was from Marie—I've no want for it now."

The porter came over to them and as he moved into the light Roger saw his brow was lined like a basket woven of wicker. He asked if they could spare a smoke and Mark obliged. Roger watched as he shuffled back across the paving, waiting until the old man was again perched on his makeshift stool before continuing.

"You know she actually said she needed to *let her creative side breathe.*"

Mark rolled his eyes. "Christ almighty. Forget Pocahontas, she sounds more like Yoko Ono." Roger chuckled, the snigger graduated into a cough as the tar tickled his throat and he covered his mouth with a fist. "And how can you take seriously anyone who goes to work in a pink wig. What is she, in disguise or something?"

Roger wiped his mouth with the back of his hand. "To tell you the truth, I kind of liked the wigs. They come in handy, you know, least they did in the beginning." He flicked ash in to the gutter. "Everyone's got to have their thing. Set themselves apart."

Mark grinned. "So Marie's thing is wigs, being delusional and a total slut." He extinguished the cigarette on the brick wall and tossed the twisted stub into the gutter. "She sure scores high on those fronts." He folded his arms across his narrow chest. "Hurry up with that," he said, "I'm starting to freeze out here."

Back in the Gamble Room their main courses were waiting for them and conversation had settled on the unveiling of a new installation at the Tate Modern. Roger removed his soggy blazer and slung it on the back of his chair; his hair was saturated and tussled, his cheeks ablaze from the change in atmospherics. Mark sat and tugged at the damp patches of his shirt around the shoulders where the cotton was almost transparent. He set to work on the lamb shank, easing the meat from the bone and covering it in gravy. Roger leaned over his plate and took a deep breath; scenting the bitter carbon he figured his steak was overdone. Across the table Marie was talking animatedly in to her phone, drawing scowls of disproval from diners at adjacent tables.

"So Serge, Guillaume," said Mark, gesturing with his fork at one and then the other. "Going for a December wedding; church-based I take it?"

"Don't be an ass," Tess said slapping him on the arm.

Serge laughed. "No Mark, it'll be in Richmond Park. You know the lodge by Ham Gate?"

"Oh Mark, you should see the view," said Tess. "You can see halfway across London from up there."

"Well, the view, it looks west," said Serge, "so you can see half of London, but it's mostly Heathrow. Maybe Staines on a clear day."

Mark took another gravy-laden bite as the table laughed. "Sounds perfect," he said.

Marie finished her call and returned her phone to the bag hung on her chair. "That was Lautrec. He's just finishing up. Should be down in about a half hour." Mark looked at Roger and raised an eyebrow.

The champagne and heavy food began to take their toll and conversation waned. Only the sound of Roger's steak knife grating against the porcelain was audible over a neighbouring table cooing as they received their crème brûlées. Roger cut a small strip from the porterhouse, pronged it with the tip of his fork and used his knife to coat the morsel with mustard; the steak was medium-well at best. Mark selected a seeded roll from the communal basket and looked across the table towards Marie. Roger knew she wasn't wearing anything beneath the body-hugging knitwear, and from the lingering nature of his friend's gaze it was apparent this was not lost on him either. Using his thumbs, Mark parted the warm doughy roll. "Marie," he said, "would you be a darl' and pass me *le buerre*." Roger sat motionless, watching his friend and girlfriend exchange creeping smiles. Obligingly, she handed him the ramekin of soft butter. Conversation resumed, flittering about Roger, and as he chewed the cindered meat, mustard burned in his throat.

Contributors

Alexa Beattie, a Londoner by birth, lives in St. Louis where her story, 'Cold Cut' is set. She has degrees in philosophy and creative writing, and is finishing a work of non-fiction.

Jon Boilard was born and raised in Western Massachusetts. He has been living and writing in Northern California since 1986. His short stories have been published in literary journals in the U.S., Canada, Europe and Asia. One was nominated for a Pushcart Prize, another received a special mention for the same, a third won the Sean O'Faolain Award and several others have earned individual small press honors. His first novel *A River Closely Watched* was published by MacAdam Cage in 2012.

Sophie Hampton was born and brought up in London. Her work has been broadcast on BBC Radio 4 and published in the *Eastern Daily Press, Scribble magazine, The Yellow Room* and digitally by Ether books. Competition successes include Bridport Prize shortlisted 2012, 2nd Prize at the Wells Festival of Literature 2011 and a finalist in the Brit Writers' Awards 2010. She is studying for an MA in creative writing at Sheffield Hallam University and is working on her first collection of short stories.

Aidan Harman writes poetry and prose, some of which has been published in *Southword* and elsewhere.

James Harkin writes for the Guardian and the Financial Times. He is the author of a book based on his columns for the *Guardian, Big Ideas: The Essential Guide To The Latest Thinking, Cyburbia: The dangerous idea that's changing how we live and who we are,* and *War Against All: The Struggle for Northern Syria,* available on Kindle

DEIRDRE JACOBSON has lived in New York City for over thirty-two years (and counting . . .), she is a native of Appalachian Virginia. In 2004 she received the Lyric Recovery Poetry Prize and was a semifinalist in the James Jones First Novel Fellowship competition. In 2005 she was a runner-up for the Sean O'Faolain Short Story Award. Most recently, she was a 2010 finalist in the fiction competitions for Inkwell, Third Coast, Nimrod (Katherine Anne Porter Prize), and the Tennessee Williams/New Orleans Literary Festival. In the same year she was also a quarter-finalist for the Nimrod Pablo Neruda Poetry Prize. Her work has appeared in *Rolling Stone, The Sow's Ear Poetry Review, Inkwell, The Spoon River Poetry Review,* and *Southword 9.*

Born in Cork, MARY LELAND has worked as a journalist, theatre and literary critic and is author of two novels; *The Killeen* (London 1985 and USA, 1986) and *Approaching Priests* (London 1991) and of T*he Little Galloway Girls* collection of short stories (London 1987). Her short fiction has been widely anthologised and *The Killeen* was selected as the Irish novel of 1985 by George O'Brien in his study *The Irish Novel, 1960 - 2010* (Cork University Press June 2012).

ANNA MAY MANGAN was born in London, where she lives and works as a feature writer for newspapers and magazines. Her first non-fiction book, *Getting into Medical School ~ The Pushy Mother's Guide* (Spine Publishing) was published in September 2008. All of her published work can be seen on her website www.annamaymangan.co.uk

BERNIE MCGILL lives in Portstewart in Northern Ireland. She is the author of *The Butterfly Cabinet* (named in 2012 by Downton creator Julian Fellowes as his novel of the year) and of *Sleepwalkers,* a collection of short stories long-listed for the 2013 Frank O'Connor International Short Story Award. She is the recipient of three Arts Council of Northern Ireland Awards. Her short fiction has been shortlisted for the Bridport, the Fish and the Michael McLaverty Short Story Prizes and she won the Zoetrope: All-Story Award in the US in 2010. She is currently working on a second novel.

Toby McGrath is a song and story writer born to the west of Dublin City in Clondalkin and now living north of the river Liffey. Along with the winning the Sean O'Faolain Prize, previous recognition includes thirteen published songs (Emma Music); an O.Z. Whitehead award (2nd place) for a one-act stage play; 'Blind Man's Bluff', a radio play broadcast on RTE, and both long and short listings in the FISH short story competition.

Alan McMonagle is a poet, playwright and short fiction writer living in Galway. He has received awards for his work from the Professional Artists' Retreat in Yaddo (New York), the Fundación Valparaiso (Spain), the Banff Centre for Creativity (Canada) and the Arts Council of Ireland. He has contributed stories to many journals in Ireland and North America including *The Adirondack Review, Natural Bridge, Grain, Prairie Fire, The Stinging Fly, Southword* and *The Penny Dreadful Magazine. Liar Liar,* his first collection of stories, appeared in 2008 (Wordsonthestreet). The title story from his second collection, *Psychotic Episodes,* (Arlen House, 2013) was nominated for a 2011 Pushcart Prize.

David Mohan is based in Dublin, and received a PhD in English literature from Trinity College. He came second in the Sean O'Faolain Short Story Prize and won the Hennessy/Sunday Tribune New Irish Writer Award. He has been published in *Necessary Fiction, Southword, Word Riot, Opium, SmokeLong Quarterly, FRiGG, Contrary, elimae, NANO, Flash International magazine, The Chattahoochee Review, New World Writing* and *Used Furniture Review.* He has been nominated for The Pushcart Prize.

James Moynihan was an engineer until MS nearly finished him off in 1998. He won the Seán O'Faoláin Prize in 2005 and placed in RTE's Francis MacManus competition. While his immune system has been trying to demolish his brain, his brain has been trying to figure out why this happens to some humans. He has been published in *The Instrument Society of America, The Tampa Review, Conduit, The Evening Echo, Whispers and Shouts, Southword, Sharp Sticks—Driven Nails,* and *Medical Hypotheses.*

Nikita Nellin, originally born in Moscow, Russia, immigrated to the U.S. in 1989. His writing often focusses on the immigration experience and the voices of American subcultures. He is the recipient of the 2010 Sean O'Faolain Short Story Prize, the 2011 SLS prize for non-fiction, and was longlisted for the 2011 Faulkner-Wisdon short story prize. Most recently he has been writing travel journalism and perspective pieces for the Hannah Arendt Center. Currently he resides in New Orleans, Louisiana.

Pat O'Connor was a winner of the 2009 Best Start Short Story Competition in Glimmertrain. In 2010, he was shortlisted for the Sean O'Faolain Short Story Prize. In 2011, he was shortlisted for the Francis MacManus Award and won the Sean O'Faolain prize. In 2012 he was shortlisted for the Hennessy New Irish Writing Award and the Fish Short Story prize. His stories have been published in the journals *Southword* and *Revival,* in the *Irish Independent,* and broadcast on RTE.

Laura Rock's fiction has appeared in Canadian journals including *The New Quarterly, The Antigonish Review, The Dalhousie Review* and *U of T Magazine* online, winning several awards. She has also published essays and poetry. A graduate of the University of Toronto (BA) and Syracuse University (MA), Rock was born and raised in the United States and later immigrated to Canada. She lives with her husband and four children in Lakefield, Ontario, where she teaches college communications and is finishing her first short story collection.

Joyce Russell is a writer, journalist, editor and teacher. She lives in the mountains of West Cork where she combines her passions for writing and gardening. Joyce is the winner of many short story competitions. A collection, *Bloodlines And Other Stories,* was published by Mercier Press in 2012. She is an editor of *Southword* and judge of the Sean O'Faolain Short Story Competition 2013/14. Other published work includes: the best-selling *Polytunnel Book*; regular features in magazines and newspapers; and contributions to radio broadcasts, literary journals and anthologies.

JULIA VAN MIDDLESWOTH is the recipient of The New Jersey Council On The Arts Fellowship as well as The Fish International Short Story Award which she won just two months before The Sean O'Faoláin Short Story Prize. She has been published in many journals including *The Literary Review* and recently finished a novel titled *Daddy Dead* based on the short story. She recently completed her MFA and will begin teaching at Middlesex Community College this fall, Julia lives with her husband, a Chihuahua, a mourning dove and a big black cat in Somerville NJ, USA.

WILLIAM WALL is the author of four novels, three collections of poetry, most recently *Ghost Estate* (Salmon Poetry) and a collection of short stories. He has won and been shortlisted for several prizes including the National Book Award. His work has been published in English and in several countries and languages. More information at his website: www.williamwall.net

THOMAS WATSON is a writer-slash-analyst living and working in his hometown, London. For the past year he has been focussing on a series of short stories and he is now concentrating on his first novel. He has read at Brixton Book Jam. He tweets, but not prolifically. He has attended creative writing classes under Maggie Hamand and Sean Levin. Thomas has lived in Japan, France and Central America. The Cafe at the V&A is his first publication.